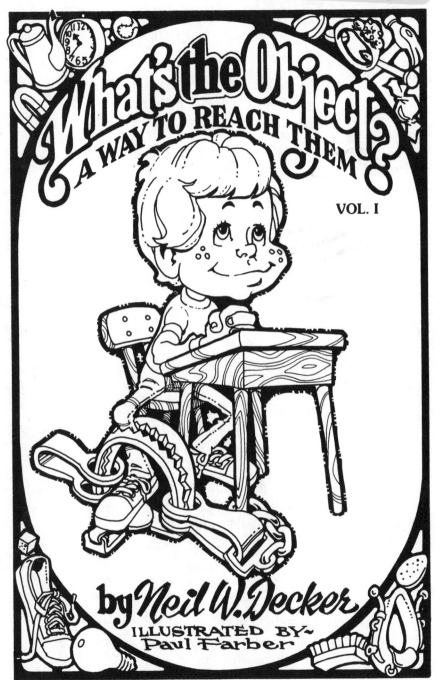

What's the Object?
A WAY TO REACH THEM

VOL. I

by Neil W. Decker

ILLUSTRATED BY~
Paul Farber

PREFACE

WHAT'S THE OBJECT?

150 Pages of exciting Learning Activities or Object lessons, illustrated and outlined step by step.

For All Teachers: Parents-Family Home Evening, Sunday School, Primary, Priesthood, MIA, Seminary & Institute.

Spice to a Lesson.

A Fun way to Teach.

A Fun way to Learn.

A Library of Unforgettable Lessons.

A way to Reach Them.

A Better way to get a Point Across.

A way to "Lead" them to water and make them Thirsty enough to drink.

A Storehouse of Lesson Motivators, Attention Getters and Clinchers.

A Book of Parables using today's problems and Familiar Objects.

As you use WHAT'S THE OBJECT? Those who hear and see you will more fully understand, remember and enjoy living the beautiful gospel truths you illustrate and demonstrate.

Teaches you how to make your own object lessons.

Lists over 200 objects used by Jesus in setting forth gospel principles.

Uses 94 gospel topics

This is for you, teacher,
wherever you are

Note: All of the Object Lessons in this book
have been used, tried, and proven in Seminary classes.

CONTENTS

ACTIVITY

OBJECTIVE:

To show we lose contact with the Lord when the gap between us gets too wide.

EQUIPMENT:

A spark plug with an extremely wide gap.

ACTIVITY AND APPLICATION

Show the spark plug, or pass it around the class. Ask: What obvious problem do you see with the spark plug? (The gap is too wide.) What is the result of an excessively wide gap? (There is no spark.) How is our church activity like the gap of a spark plug? (Student choice.) What happens when the spiritual gap between us and the Lord gets too wide? (Student choice.) How do we keep our spiritual gap close? (Student choice.) Through prayer, service, church activity, obedience and scripture study, we are kept close to the spirit of the Lord.

APOSTASY

OBJECTIVE:

To show how individual apostasy begins.

EQUIPMENT:

A banana that has been cut in half in the inside, by using a needle and thread as illustrated.

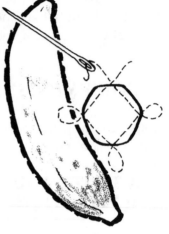

ACTIVITY AND APPLICATION:

Show the banana to the class and ask a student to examine it. Now have the student peel the banana and show the class that it is cut in half. Ask: How did this happen? (Student choice.) How does this illustration compare with how and why some members leave the faith? (Student choice.) How does individual apostasy begin? (Student choice.) The first step to apostasy starts when we begin criticizing or cutting down our leaders. The church is hurt very little by outside forces, the damage is done within.

ATONEMENT

OBJECTIVE:

To illustrate the meaning of the atonement in a simple manner.

EQUIPMENT:

A set of balance scales, two small nice-looking good oranges, one medium orange that is hard and all dried up. The two small oranges need to balance each other on the scales.

ACTIVITY AND APPLICATION:

Tell the class that this demonstration represents the atonement; you look for the applications. Put one good orange on one side of the scale and ask: How does this represent sin in the atonement. (Adam's transgression and our sins.) Put the dry orange on the other side and ask: Why doesn't it balance? (Student choice.) What might this represent in the atonement? (No repentance.) The Lord's atonement has no effect because there has been no repentance. Now replace the dry orange with the other good one, and the scale will balance. Why does it balance? (Student choice.) What in the atonement does this represent? (Christ' atonement and our faith and repentance.) According to Alma 11:40; 34:14-16 and D&C 19:16, who receives the blessings of Christ' redemption? (Only those who believe and repent.)

BLESSINGS

OBJECTIVE:

To demonstrate how the Lord returns blessings unto us for what we give.

EQUIPMENT:

A sack and a one dollar bill.

ACTIVITY AND APPLICATION:

Show the sack and the dollar bill and ask: If someone told you that you could have all the dollar bills that this sack would hold, how would you put them in the sack? (Student choice.) According to Luke 6:38, how does this compare with the way the Lord blesses us for giving? (He said: "Give, and it shall be given unto you; good measure, pressed down, and shaken together, and running over..." Luke 6:38.)

BOOK OF MORMON

OBJECTIVE:

To show how important the Book of Mormon is.

EQUIPMENT:

A boat anchor.

ACTIVITY AND APPLICATION:

Hang a large anchor from the ceiling, so the class can see it. Ask: Why do we use anchors? (Student choice.) What will an anchor do? (Student choice.) Make the following statement: It has been said that the Book of Mormon is an anchor to our faith. What do you think that means? (Student choice.) If we know the Book of Mormon is true, how will it anchor our faith? (It will keep us from drifting away from the faith when we run into hardships and the waves of life get rough.) If the Book of Mormon is true, what conclusions can we make? (1. Joseph Smith was a true prophet. 2. The Church which was organized through him is the true Church of Jesus Christ.)

CARING

OBJECTIVE:

To illustrate how we can bring out the very best in people.

EQUIPMENT:

Popcorn, popped and unpopped.

ACTIVITY AND APPLICATION:

Show a glass of popcorn kernels. Quote the following poem:
> "The first time you notice me you'll have to admit,
> I Have an outside hard as grit.
> No amount of force or pressure
> can make me change to something better.
> But if by a gentle flame I'm basted,
> I'll change to the best eating popcorn you've ever tasted.
> (show some nice fluffy popped popcorn.)
> Some people are like popcorn too--
> with an outside shell that's hard to get through.
> But if you take the time to care,
> you'll discover the potential hidden there.
> Through unselfish service you can help others grow,
> by taking the time to let your love show."
> -- Joan Salgy

How are people like popcorn? (Student choice.) How can we get through to hardcrusted people.? (People, like popcorn, have a great beautiful potential. When warmed they respond and open up to reveal their greatness.)

CHARACTER

OBJECTIVE:

To show how character, the inner part of us is damaged when we remove our protective coating of righteous living by sinning.

EQUIPMENT:

Potato peeler, two potatoes: One with the peel still on, and the other one with the peeling removed. Peel the one about two days prior to use, it will turn black.

ACTIVITY AND APPLICATION:

Show the potato that has not been peeled. What is a potato like under the peeling? (Clean and white.) Why can't we remove some of the peeling without harming it? (Student choice.) Now remove some of the peeling with the potato peeler. What will happen to this unprotected potato? (It will go black.) Show the second potato, the one that is black. Ask: How did it get black? (When the protective coating is removed from the potato the inside becomes black.) In this same way, how are people like potatoes? (Student response.) What is our protective coating? (Righteous living.) How does our protective coating get removed? (By sinning.) What happens when our protective coating of righteous living is removed through sin? (Our inner character is darkened.) Sometimes we think we can sin a little and no harm is done.

CHASTITY

OBJECTIVE:

To demonstrate how the clean and unspotted will ring true to their ideals.

EQUIPMENT:

A bell and some play modeling clay.

ACTIVITY AND APPLICATION:

Ring the bell to show the clarity of the tone. What is the sound of a bell like? (It is clear, sharp and loud.) Now stick some globs of clay on two or three spots around the outside of the bell. Ring the bell again and ask: What is the difference in its ring this time? (Student choice.) How is immoral conduct like the clay on the bell? (When a clean and true person becomes spotted by the things of the world they do not ring true to their ideals.) How does what we do on the outside affect the inside? (Student choice.)

CHASTITY

OBJECTIVE:

To illustrate how Satan enters into our lives.

EQUIPMENT:

A big box labeled "My Life", with a door labeled "No Trespassing." A shoe cut out of cardboard.

ACTIVITY AND APPLICATION:

Show the box and ask: What do you think this box means? (It represents your life.) What is the only way evil can ever get inside? (Through the door.) How could the devil get through the door? (It is extremely difficult, if not impossible, for the devil to enter a door that is closed. He seems to have no keys for locked doors.) So what happens if the door is left ajar? (Satan will try to get in.) How does immorality get its start? (Student choice.) Use the shoe to demonstrate getting the foot in the door when it is left open. What are some things that leave the door open? (Immodesty, improper dating, and general disobedience.) What happens when the devil gets his toe in? (Then he gets his foot, leg and his all in.)

CHILD LIKE FAITH

OBJECTIVE:

To illustrate the Lord's statement; "Except ye be converted, and become as lit-
tle children, ye shall not
enter into the kingdom of
heaven." Matt. 18:3.

EQUIPMENT:

Chalk board and chalk.

ACTIVITY AND APPLICATION:

Write the following on the chalk board and cover it until
you want it seen: "God is Nowhere." Ask the class to
look at what you're going to show them, read it and
decide what it says. Now uncover the statement and ask:
What does it say? (Student choice.) Why did some of
you read it: God is No Where? (Student choice.) Now
tell the following story and demonstrate it on the chalk
board as you do so. It is said that a cobbler who was an
infidel wrote on a blackboard in his shoe shop: "God is
nowhere." A little girl, who had just learned to read,
came into his place of business soon after, took a look at
the statement on the board and then slowly picked up
the chalk, and placing a line made it to read God is
Now/here. What quality did the little girl demonstrate?
(Faith in the Lord Jesus Christ.) According to Matt. 18:3,
why must we also demonstrate this kind of faith? ("Except ye be converted, and become as little children, ye
shall not enter into the kingdom of heaven."

COMMUNISM AND SATAN

OBJECTIVE:

To show how Satan works to get our people to accept his philosophies, such as communism.

EQUIPMENT:

Two large animal traps — one is in very good working condition and has a good strong spring. The other one looks good when it is set, but it's spring has no power; two pieces of candy one small and one large, as illustrated.

ACTIVITY AND APPLICATION:

Prior to class tape a small piece of candy to the trigger of the bad trap, and a big piece to the good trap. Set both traps. Pick up the bad trap and explain that any one can have the candy if they can get it out of the trap with their hand. They must get it with their hand only by going down through the top of the trap. If no one will do it, pick someone and promise him that he will not be harmed in any way because the trap does not work. Let him get the candy. Now pick up the good trap and give the students the same instruction, except tell them that this trap really works. When no one will try for

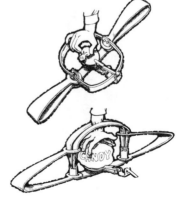

the candy, demonstrate what would happen to the student's finger if he got it caught in this trap. Put a pencil in the trap setting off the trigger. Replace the large candy on the trigger, reset the trap and challenge someone to get the candy in the same manner as the first. How is Satan's plan of communism like this illustration? (Student choice.) Why do they give us a little without hurting us? (It makes us go after more.) How does Satan entice us with communism? (He entices us by feeding us little bits of socialism in a friendly unharmful manner, we get a little of something for nothing, and little by little we desire the bigger. And then we really get hurt and lose our freedoms.)

CONTENTION

OBJECTIVE:

To show that many problems coming at you all at once, are difficult to handle.

EQUIPMENT:

Three or four balls (sponge or ping pong)

ACTIVITY AND APPLICATION:

With advance notice throw one ball to an athletic-type boy. Then without notice throw three or four balls one after another or all at once to the same boy. Most or all of the balls will be missed. Why couldn't he catch them? (Student choice.) When are pressures the hardest to handle? (We can cope with problems and pressures one at a time, but when they come all at once, handling any of them is very difficult.) Concentrate on solving one problem at a time even though they seem to come all at once.

CONVERSION

OBJECTIVE:

To illustrate how true conversion to the gospel means total acceptance of its teachings.

EQUIPMENT:

A candle or kerosene lamp and a small 10 watt light bulb and socket.

ACTIVITY AND APPLICATION:

Turn off all the class room lights. Tell the following story and demonstrate as you go: After electricity had just become available for homes, a farmer who had been accustomed to just candle or kerosene light, (now turn on the lamp or light the candle) and who had done all his reading and everything by it, resisted the change to electricity. He finally agreed to let his house be wired for power. As a selling point, the salesman told him that with electric power, the house could be as light at midnight as it was at noon. So the contract was signed and the wiring completed. (Turn off the lamp or blow out the

candle and turn on the 10 watt bulb.) Sometime later the salesman was riding around the area after dark and noticed that the farmer's house didn't look any brighter than it did while he was using kerosene lamp or candle light. He decided to investigate, and found the wiring was alright. Ask: What do you think his problem was? (The fault was in the light bulbs. The farmer was using 10 watt bulbs.) How are members of the church sometimes like the farmer? (Student choice.) What is the potential of a person who accepts the gospel and receives the Holy Ghost? (Student choice.) The Lord wired us for 120 volts capable of burning hundreds of watts, but how are we sometimes more foolish than the farmer? (Student choice.) If we only use a fraction of the spiritual wattage available to us we are no wiser than the farmer who was using 10 watt bulbs.

DEPENDABILITY

OBJECTIVE:

To illustrate how we can stick to our task until it sticks to us.

EQUIPMENT:

A stamped card or envelope.

ACTIVITY AND APPLICATION:

Show the stamped envelope and ask: In what way can we be like the postage stamp? (Student choice.) Then quote the following poem:

"There was a little postage stamp,
  no bigger than your thumb,
but still it stuck right on the job
  until it's work was done.
They licked it and they pounded it
  till it would make you sick.
But the more it took the lickin,
  why, the tighter it would stick.
Let's be like that postage stamp,
  in playing life's big game,
and stick to what we know is right,
  and then we can't miss our aim."
  --Author unknown

What are the qualities of a postage stamp? (It always stays on the job until it completes its assignment.) So how can we be like the postage stamp? (It doesn't matter how big you are, or the job you're called to do, do it until it's finished. You may be abused and take a beating, but as long as you know you're right you will reach your goal.)

DISCIPLINE

OBJECTIVE:

To demonstrate why children and students need discipline.

EQUIPMENT:

Cow hobbles.

ACTIVITY AND APPLICATION:

Show the hobbles and ask: What are these? Why do farmers use them? (They stop the cow from kicking.) What is the best thing a cow has to offer? (Milk.) How can we hobble our children or our students? (By discipline.) Why do we put hobbles on them? (We put hobbles on cows so we can get the very best out of them.) Students like cows have a lot to offer with their

great potential, so we put hobbles on them, in the way of restrictions and discipline, so we can get the very best out of them. A label on a milk bottle read: "Our cows are not content, they strive to do better".

DOING

OBJECTIVE:

To illustrate the difference between a member of the church who really is converted and lives his religion and one who just goes through the motions.

EQUIPMENT:

A glass of water, a coin and an Alka-Seltzer.

ACTIVITY AND APPLICATION:

Watch this demonstration and observe how it is like members of the church. Show the glass of water, the coin and the Alka-Seltzer. The glass of water represents the gospel, the coin and the Alka-Seltzer represent members of the church. Drop the coin in the water first and then drop in the Alka-Seltzer. Ask: How are some members like the coin? (They enter the church with a splash, and go right through all its programs: Primary, Sunday School, MIA, Seminary, and Institute.) What kind of member does the Alka-Seltzer represent? (Student choice.) This person also goes through the programs of the church, but what happens to this person that did not happen to the first one? (He not only goes through the programs of the church but the church goes through him: he just bubbles with enthusiasm.) As we live the gospel by doing, all its great programs become a part of our lives and we become one.

18

DO'S - CAUTIONS - DON'TS

OBJECTIVE:

To demonstrate and compare David's moral downfall, II Samuel 11, with today so we will not make the same mistake.

EQUIPMENT:

Signal light, ask your county highway department, or make one with red, yellow, and green lights.

ACTIVITY AND APPLICATION:

As you start to teach this lesson, turn on all three lights at once and ask: If you came to an intersection and saw this, what would you do? (Student choice.) What would be the best thing to do? Stop and use caution. With the use of this light we will demonstrate how cautious we must be in life. Turn off all the lights. Now turn on the green light. What is the meaning of this light? Proceed on course. How was David's life like the green light? He was a real goer. He had killed a lion and a bear, was a shepherd, played

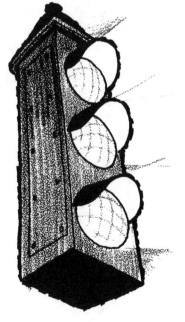

the harp for the king, killed Goliath and became king of Israel, and all this before age thirty. How can you become a real goer like David? (Student choice.) Where must we go? On a mission, marry in the covenant and get an education. Turn off the green light and turn on the yellow light and ask: What is the meaning of this light? Proceed with caution. What cautions should David have taken? II Samuel 11:1,2. As king, he should have been in the right place, out to battle. Next, when he saw the woman bathing, what light should he have used? (Student choice.) He should have fled in a hurry. What cautions must we use today when we get in a similar situation? (Student choice.) Turn off the yellow light and turn on the red light. What is it's meaning? What were the stops that David should have heeded? II Samuel 11:3,4. He had no business inquiring about the woman or sending for her, because they each had a spouse. What are the stops that we must heed today in order to avoid falling into sin as David did? (Student choice.)

EDUCATION

OBJECTIVE:

To demonstrate the folly of putting off education.

EQUIPMENT:

A dull ax, and a grindstone.

ACTIVITY AND APPLICATION:

Show the ax and the grindstone and ask: What do you think of the wood chopper who thinks he can't afford to stop chopping long enough to sharpen his ax? (Student choice.) Now actually sharpen the ax on the grindstone and ask: Why is it wise to stop and sharpen the ax or saw? (Student choice.) What about the boy who says he can't afford to quit his good paying job to finish his education? (Student choice.) How are the boy and the wood cutter's mistakes similar? (The boy who drops out of school, under the delusion that the money he can earn will be worth more to him than an education, makes as fatal a mistake as does the wood chopper who thinks he can't afford to stop chopping long enough to sharpen his ax. The difference between meeting life's problems with a trained mind and a dull mind is even greater than the difference between chopping wood with a sharp ax and a dull one.)

EQUALITY

OBJECTIVE:

To illustrate the feeling that is caused by inequality.

EQUIPMENT:

The following five kinds of candy: One large candy bar, one regular sized candy bar, one small candy bar, one tootsie roll, one little M&M or equivalent, and five additional tootsie rolls.

ACTIVITY AND APPLICATION:

Invite five students to come to the front of the class. Now explain: I would like you to take the role of being my five children. I have something for each of you to show my joy and appreciation for you. Now pass out the pieces of candy starting biggest candy bar down to the littlest piece. There may be some obvious expressions of inequality, if so use them for your discussion. Ask: How do you feel about your reward? (Student choice.) If this really did happen to you in your family, how would you feel? (Student choice.) Ask the whole class how they would feel if this happened to them. (Student choice.) Now collect all the candy that you gave them and give all five of the students a tootsie roll. What is the difference in your feelings now? (Student choice.) Why do you feel better when you all received equal amounts? (Student choice.) Let the five students keep the tootsie roll and return to their seats. A great example of this is in 4 Nephi: 1,2,3,15 and 16, when they had all things in common and there never were a happier people.

EXPECTATIONS

OBJECTIVE:

To demonstrate how expecta-
tions change when we permit
things to change our potential.

EQUIPMENT:

One egg with its inside colored
with food coloring. Inject it with a hypodermic needle.

ACTIVITY AND APPLICATION:

Show the egg. Now tell me everything you know about an
egg. (Student choice.) What are its uses? What is the egg's
potential? Describe an egg. What would you expect to find
inside an egg? How do you know all this about an egg?
(Student choice.) Now crack the egg open and watch the
reaction. What changed the eggs contents? (Student
choice.) We are born to be someone special, a child of
God. Why do we sometimes become less than our potential? (Student choice.) What do some people let enter into
themselves that changes our expectation of them? (Student choice.) It has been said that:
  "All the water in all the world,
      no matter how hard it tried,
   could never sink the smallest ship, unless it got inside.
   And all the evil in all the word,
      the blackest kind of sin,
   could never hurt you the least little bit unless you let
      it in."
   Author unknown.

23

FAITH – HOPE – CHARITY

OBJECTIVE:

To demonstrate the relationship between Faith, Hope and Charity.

EQUIPMENT:

An old pitcher pump, a two quart bottle full of water, and an old baking powder can.

ACTIVITY AND APPLICATION:

Set the old pitcher pump along with the bottle of water and the baking powder can in front of the class. Let's assume you were crossing a desert under a hot blistering sun, and you came upon a water pump. You get closer and you notice a bottle of water. What would be your first impulse? (Drink the water.) Then you notice a note stuck in a baking powder can. "This pump is old, the note began, but she works, so give her a try." Now what are your alternatives? (Drink the water or pour it in the pump.) If you drink the water, what would it be like? (Hot and stale.) What principle would you have to exercise in order to pour the water down the pump? (Faith.) What evidence do you have that gives you hope that there's water? (The pump, the note, and the water.) Why does the

water have to be poured down the pump? (To prime it.) What is required as soon as you pour the water in the pump? (Work, you must work the handle like there's a fire; pump like mad.) If you follow the directions and work hard, what will be your reward? (Fresh water, all you can drink, and enough to wash from head to feet.) After you get all you want, what should you do? (Leave the bottle full for others.) What gospel principle does this represent? (Charity.)

FAMILY

OBJECTIVE:

To show that when the family is right the world will be also.

EQUIPMENT:

A map of the world, with a picture of a family on the back of it.

ACTIVITY AND APPLICATION:

Tell the following story and show the map in the proper place: A father was busy preparing his income tax on the deadline day. His young son kept asking him many questions. Finally disgusted with this, the father ripped a big page out of the world book. On it was a map of the world. (Show the map side of the page.) He then ripped it into small pieces and gave it to his son, saying, "Now go put this picture of the world together like a puzzle." The father thought all would be well for quite a while. But to his surprise, the boy returned in ten minutes with the map of the world all put together. The dad asked his son; "How could you put it together so fast?" "Easy," replied the boy. "On the back of the map (show the picture of the family on the other side) was a picture of a family, I knew if the family was right, the world had to be." What are some gospel applications? (Student choice.) How important is the family unit? (If the family is right, the world is also. The family is the most important unit in the whole world.)

FATHER

OBJECTIVE:

To illustrate the importance of taking time with your children.

EQUIPMENT:

An apple peeling device, a pocket knife, and two nice firm apples.

ACTIVITY AND APPLICATION:

Relate the following story as you peel an apple with the pocket knife: A lady tells this story with tears in her eyes. She remembers when she was young, how her father would come in the house after a hard day's work on the farm, take the newspaper and four or five big apples, go into the living room, sit down and peel an apple from start to finish in one piece without breaking the peeling. We would gather around in amazement at his skill. All the while he was peeling the apple he would be telling us stories about when he was growing up and other lessons of life. After he finished one apple, he would cut it into sections and give each of us kids a piece. He would never eat very much of the apple himself. Now take the apple peeling device and show how we do it today. Show how it

can peel and slice an apple in one process in less than one minute. In the story, what do you think the father's main objective was? (Student choice.) What gave the kids the greatest joy? (It wasn't the apples that the kids enjoyed so much, as it was that the father took time to be with them and share life-lasting experiences with them.)

FIRST DAY CHALLENGE

OBJECTIVE:

Use for fun the first day of class to challenge students to make this a great class.

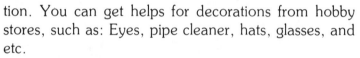

EQUIPMENT:

Five potatoes decorated up like those in the illustration. You can get helps for decorations from hobby stores, such as: Eyes, pipe cleaner, hats, glasses, and etc.

ACTIVITY AND APPLICATION:

Show a big potato and ask: What are some other names for this? (Spuds and taters.) Well let's talk about taters. Let's pretend that this is a class of taters. Let's see what kind of taters we have in this class. Now show each one of the decorated potatoes one at a time and ask the class to identify each tater and give characteristics of each.

First the SPECTATOR. Ask: What tater is this? (Spectator.) What does a spectator do in class? (He just sits and watches and doesn't get involved.)

Second the AGITATOR. Ask: What tater is this? (Agitator.) What is the main pupose of an agitator? (He always gives you a bad time.)

Third the COMMONTATOR. Ask: What kind of tater is this? (Common tater.) What does it mean to be common? (Just an ordinary average student.)

Fourth the ANTICIPATATOR. Ask: What tater does this represent? (Anticipatator.) What would an anticipatator always do? (Would always look forward to coming to calss.)

Fifth the PARTICIPATATOR. Ask: What would this tater be? (Participatator.) Why is this one the most valuable? (He gets involved in an active positive way and is self motivated.) Which of these taters should we mash from our class? (Student choice.)

FOLLOW THE PROPHET

OBJECTIVE:

To show how people are led away by man-made prophets.

EQUIPMENT:

Compass, a small magnet.

ACTIVITY AND APPLICATION:

Show the compass and ask a student to come up and read the compass. Ask him to point in the direction of north according to the compass. Now go up close to the compass, with the magnet in your hand and ask: What direction is north? Why did it change? (Because of the magnet.) How does a compass work? (By the magnetic pull of the North Pole.) How far away do you think the North Pole is? (Student choice.) Even though it is thousands of miles away, why is it's power still felt. (Student choice.) What did I use to change its direction? (A man made magnet that is closer.) What powerful force do we have in our church that is likened to the magnetic pull of the North Pole? (A living Prophet.) A living Prophet, even though thousands of miles away has the power to influence us. What causes us to lose our direction? (We permit evil forces which are closer to us to lead us away.)

FORGIVENESS-CONFESSION

OBJECTIVE:

To illustrate the joy and the miracle of forgiveness as described in Alma 36: 16-21 and Isaiah 1:18.

EQUIPMENT:

An old white bone, and a brown bone that has been buried.

ACTIVITY AND APPLICATION:

Show the two bones and ask: What is the difference between these two bones? (Student choice.) How did the light one get white? (From the sun.) Why isn't this other bone white? (It has been buried.) What is the best way for us to get rid of our sins? (Get them out in the open.) What happens when we hide our sins? (Quote the following poem:)

If the sea	Oh, how bright	and how calm
And the sun	my soul	and warm
can bleach a bone	can emerge, purged	his sand.
til' it's whiter	on the beach	
than a gull,	of Christ' water	Author unknown
cleaner than foam	and light	

As the bone is bleached white by the miracle of nature, so also can man's sins and mistakes be forgiven through the miracle of forgiveness.

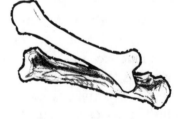

FREEDOM

OBJECTIVE:

To demonstrate the cycle
from bondage to freedom.
Mosiah 21:5-15.

EQUIPMENT:

Handcuffs, good official ones with a key.

ACTIVITY AND APPLICATION:

Handcuff a boy to something solid. Say: You may try
any method you can think of to get yourself out of the
bondage you're in. As you're thinking of ways to get
out, listen to our discussion as we read some suggestions from the scriptures. They may give you some
clues on how to get free. Go over the scripture insights
from the following scriptures: Moisiah 21:5-15 about
the many attempts of the Nephites, to get out of bondage. Any time during the scripture insights that the
student asks you for the key, give it to him. Throw it to
him so he has to work to reach it with his foot, and then
he has to unlock the handcuffs himself. Mosiah 21:13,
14 shows how they finally humbled themselves and
asked the Lord for help. Mosiah 21:15 and chapter 22
show how the Lord blessed them by helping them find
a way but they had to work it out themselves. From our
demonstration with the student and the scriptures,
what are the steps in the cycle of captivity to freedom?
(Turning to the Lord for help, then we receive help
when we are willing to work it out ourselves.)

GATHERING OF ISRAEL

OBJECTIVE:

To illustrate how the sift-
ing of the pure in heart oc-
curs.

EQUIPMENT:

a few
kernels of
corn,
wheat,
& rice

Flour sifter, a glass bowl
half full of white flour with
a few kernels of corn,
wheat and rice mixed in it.

ACTIVITY AND APPLICATION:

Show the bowl of white flour to the class. Now dump
the contents of the bowl into the flour sifter. Sift the
flour back into the glass bowl, leaving the kernels of
grain in the sifter. How is this like the gathering of Israel
and missionary work? (Student choice.) Which people
are being gathered? (Many of the chosen people are
ready now to be sifted and brought into the gospel; all
they need is a chance to hear the message of the
gospel. Others have the same potential of being sifted,
but it will take a little grinding on them before they will
be ready.)

GOALS

OBJECTIVE:

To demonstrate the value of stretching yourself to accomplish any goal.

EQUIPMENT:

Two large balloons.

ACTIVITY AND APPLICATION:

Show the two balloons before they're blown up. These balloons represent two people. Blow one of them up until it gets large. Now let the air out of it and ask: What is the difference in these two balloons now? (Student choice.) How are some people like the balloon that was not blown up? (They are content to remain as they are; they do not take the chance of expanding for fear of breaking.) How are others like the balloon that was blown up? (They stretch themselves in reaching for a goal.) As demonstrated with the balloons, what happens when we expand ourselves to reach a goal? (Once having stretched they will never be the original size again.) You will be a different person after stretching yourself to reach a goal.

GOALS

OBJECTIVE:

To illustrate the power that comes through the concentration of all our efforts upon reaching one main goal.

EQUIPMENT:

A funnel, pop bottle, bottle of water and strainer made by punching holes in the bottom of a can.

ACTIVITY AND APPLICATION:

Demonstrate the following: Show the bottle of water. It represents our efforts. Next put the funnel into the pop bottle and pour the water into it. Now empty the water from the pop bottle, back into the original bottle. Now place the strainer can over the top of the pop bottle and pour the water into it. According to our illustration, which one represents the best method of reaching our goal? (Student choice.) How are some goals like the strainer method? (Don't scatter your shots.) It is a lot better to do one thing to the best of your ability than to run second in a dozen things. When you concentrate all your efforts on one goal the results are outstanding.

GOVERNMENT

OBJECTIVE:

To illustrate the purpose of government.

EQUIPMENT:

An old washboard.

ACTIVITY AND APPLICATION:

Show the scrub board and ask: What is this? What is this board's main pupose? To clean clothes. In comparing this scrub board with todays modern washing machines, what one thing has not changed? (Its purpose.) What if things got really tough, and we didn't have electrical power to run these modern washing machines? What could we always do? (Go back to the original scrub board.) How is this scrub board like government? (Student choice.) What is the basic purpose of government? (Help keep society clean.) The basic purpose of both government and the washboard have not changed. Why have some changes been made in both? (To streamline and handle large numbers of people.) What is there about government that gives us hope and faith? (We could go back to the original basic design and still get the job done. In fact we could cut off a lot of unnecessary machinery in both the modern washing machines and modern government and still get the job done.)

GREED

OBJECTIVE:

To illustrate the folly of seeking for wealth and power.

EQUIPMENT:

A large mouth two quart jar with a ring, and candy in wrappers as illustrated.

ACTIVITY AND APPLICATION:

Take the ring and find a student whose hand will just go through, not too tight and not too loose. Bring the selected student in front of the class and tell him that he can grab all the candy he can hold in his hand, and that he can have all he can get out of the bottle without dropping any. But if he drops one piece he doesn't get any candy. What happens if we get greedy? (Student choice.) What happens when we seek for power and material things so much? (Student choice.) In Alma 46 there is a man by the name of Amalikiah whose quest for wealth and power ended with his own destruction.

HABIT

OBJECTIVE:

To illustrate how habits are hard to break.

EQUIPMENT:

Chalk and chalk board.

ACTIVITY AND APPLICATION:

Write the word H A B I T on the board in large letters. Ask: Why are habits so hard to break? (Student choice.) Now demonstrate why it is so hard to get rid of a habit.

You can take off the "H" and you still have "abit."

You can take off the "A" and you still have "bit."

You can take off the "B" and you still have "it."

Why is it so hard to get rid of a bad habit? (Student choice.) Someone has said: "Pick your ruts carefully, because you will be in them for a long time." What do you think they meant. (Student choice.)

39

HARDNESS OF HEART

OBJECTIVE:

To illustrate what it takes to soften some hard-hearted people.

EQUIPMENT:

A military ammo cartridge; two shell points, one regular lead point, and one armor piercing point: and a lead point that has been fired against something hard, so it is smashed.

ACTIVITY AND APPLICATION:

Show the smashed lead and ask: What is this? Why is it smashed? Because it hit a hard object. Now show the inside of an armor piercing bullet. Armor piercers were developed to pierce through steel in tanks and other heavy equipment. They are made from highly tempered steel. How are people like steel tanks? (Student choice.) How can we pierce through the spiritually hardened person? (The Lord developed a type of armor piercer that will penetrate through the hardest person. For example in Helaman 10:15 when the Nephites hardened their hearts, the Lord gave Nephi an armor piercer in the way of great power, power to cause a famine. Helaman 11:4,7 shows how the people softened their hearts and turned unto the Lord when they were about to perish by famine.)

HARDSHIPS

OBJECTIVE:

Demonstrate how some people have the ability to endure hardship and hang on to the finish.

EQUIPMENT:

Fork, spoon, pop bottle and a large wooden match set up as illustrated.

ACTIVITY AND APPLICATION:

Prior to class, soak the non-match end in water about half way. Connect the spoon and fork together, and balance them on the pop bottle by using the match as illustrated. The match represents people. Now light the match end with another match, and let it burn until it goes out. The fire represents the hardships and obstacles of this life. Ask: What happened? (Student choice.) How is this demonstration like enduring hardships in this life. We all receive trials equal to our ability to endure. The test of our strength is in our ability to endure them.

HOLY GHOST

OBJECTIVE:

To compare the workings of a radio with communication through the Holy Ghost.

EQUIPMENT:

A radio labeled "Holy Ghost" as illustrated.

ACTIVITY AND APPLICATION:

Show the radio and ask: What makes a radio work? (Student choice.) Plug in the radio and turn it on, but don't have it tuned. Turn up the volume without tuning it and ask: What indications are there that this radio works? (The tubes light up and it makes noise.) Why doesn't it play? (It's not tuned.) How do you tune it? (The dial must be in the proper position.) Tune it and get the reception coming in loud and clear. Now pull one of the tubes and say: This is just one little insignificant tube, why does it make so much difference? (Student choice.) Replace the tube. If we can pick up radio sound waves all around the world, what can we do with the power of the Holy Ghost? (Student choice.) But like the radio, what is the first thing we must do? (Get in tune.) How do we get in tune? (We must be in the proper position with the Lord.) In receiving the

42

Holy Ghost, what is each of the radio tubes likened to? (Commandments we must live in order to have the blessing of receiving the Holy Ghost. The prayer tube, Word of Wisdom tube, tithing tube, morality tube, and Sabbath tube. If any one of these is not working there will be no reception.)

HONESTY

OBJECTIVE:

You must be honest with
yourself.

EQUIPMENT:

Several mirrors.

ACTIVITY AND APPLICATION:

Use some mirrors so each student can look into one. Ask:
As you look into the mirror, what do you see? Do you see
what others see? How would you like to look to others?
Now give the following poem:
> "When you get what you want in your struggle for gain,
>   and the world makes you king for a day,
> Just go to the mirror and look at yourself
>   and see what that man has to say.
> It isn't your father or mother or wife,
>   whose judgment upon you must pass,
> the one whose verdict counts most in your life
>   is the one staring back in the glass.
> He's the one you must satisfy beyond all the rest,
>   for he's with you right up to the end;
> and you have passed your most difficult test
>   if the man in the glass is your friend!
> You may be one who got a good break--
>   then say I'm a wonderful guy;
> but the man in the glass says you're only a fake;
>   if you can't look him straight in the eye.
> You may fool the world down your pathway of years,

and get pats on the back as you pass;
but your final reward will be heartaches and
  tears if you've cheated the man in the glass."
    Author unknown.
Who must you satisfy most? (Student choice.) Why?
How do you cheat the man in the glass? (Student choice.)

HOT OR COLD

OBJECTIVE:

To demonstrate the Lord's statement in Revelations 3:15,16, in reference to being "Hot or Cold", but not "Luke Warm."

EQUIPMENT:

A container of the following:
Very hot water, ice cold water and luke warm water.

ACTIVITY AND APPLICATION:

Call a student to the front of the class and blindfold him. Ask the class to observe what happens. Tell the student that you are going to put his hand in some water, and that he should leave it in only as long as it is comfortable. Now let the student put his hand in the three containers in the following order: First the hot, and then the cold and last the warm. Remove the blindfold from the student and ask the class which of the three containers they think caused the least reaction? (Student choice.) Why? Now ask the student how he reacted to each container of water. What do you think the Lord meant when he said: "...be hot or cold..but not luke warm..." Revelations 3:15, 16? (Student choice.) What do hot and cold water cause us to do? (To be uncomfortable enough to get moving.) What happens to us when we are in nice warm water? (We are just content to stay where we are. We become slothful because of the easiness of the way. Alma 37:46.)

HYPOCRISY

OBJECTIVE:

To illustrate the definition of hypocrisy.

EQUIPMENT:

A nice clean shirt. Paint it and write all over it everywhere except the collar and the front middle section.

ACTIVITY AND APPLICATION:

Introduce this topic by going through the following discussion: How important is appearance? (Student choice.) What do nice neat clothes have to do with appearance? (Student choice.) Tell me honestly, do my clothes look alright for my position as your teacher? Now remove your coat and watch the reaction. This illustration is a clue to our topic. What do you think it is? (Hypocrisy.) What is a hypocrit? (Student choice.) In I Samuel 16:7, what do you think is meant by the statement: "The Lord looketh not on the outward appearance, but on the heart?" (Student choice.) Many people give an outward appearance of being clean and pure, but like the shirt, what are they like? (Student choice.)

HYPOCRISY

OBJECTIVE:

To illustrate the Lord's statement to the Scribes and Pharisees: "...ye make clean the outside of the cup and of the platter, but within they are full of extortion and excess." Matt. 23:25.

EQUIPMENT:

A platter with a lot of excess food remaining on it. Prepare a day in advance, from a platter used in a meal.

ACTIVITY AND APPLICATION:

Show the plate to the class and ask students to describe what they see. How would it make you feel if someone compared you to a dirty platter? (Student choice.) What do you think the Lord meant when he told the Scribes and Pharisees: You are like this plate, clean on the outside, but on the inside you are dirty and full of excess? (Student choice.) How do we become full of excess? (Student choice.) In what ways do we make the outside clean? (Student choice.) What makes the inside dirty? (Student choice.)

INFLUENCE

OBJECTIVE:

To show how we must put a person in the position to be influenced by the gospel.

EQUIPMENT:

Two pint bottles, a laminated card, food coloring, hot water and cold water.

ACTIVITY AND APPLICATION:

Set up the demonstration as follows: Put food coloring in the hot water, and place the card over the mouth of the hot bottle, then place the mouth of the hot bottle over the mouth of the cold bottle. Now remove the card. Ask: Why doesn't the water mix? (Heat rises.) Now reverse the position of the bottles by holding the mouth of both bottles with one hand and turn them over so the hot water is on the bottom. Now the colored water will mix. Ask: Why does the water mix? (Cold water is heavier than hot water and heat rises.) The hot water represents the gospel or high spirituality, and the cold water represents low spirituality. How is the best way to help a person of low spirituality become influenced by a person of high spirituality? (Put him in a position where he can be influenced by the gospel.) According to this illustration, what will a spiritual

49

person never do? (He will never lower his standard to the nonspiritual level.) The gospel has the power to influence anyone for good, but what must the person be willing to do in order to be influenced? (He must be willing to put himself in the position to be influenced.)

INFUSION

OBJECTIVE:

To show how one gets rid
of evil and replaces it with
righteousness through the
process of infusion as
described in Alma 19:6.

EQUIPMENT:

A little plastic or wood
carved image of a man,
some blue food coloring, an Alka-Seltzer, a bottle,
some bleach and some water.

ACTIVITY AND APPLICATION:

Put the little image of a man in the bottom of the bottle
and cover it with blue food coloring. What does this
represent? (A man in the depths of sin.) Add one Alka-
Seltzer and a cup of water that has ⅓ part bleach to the
glass with the image of the man. What do you think
this represents? (Student choice.) What happened to
the man according to Alma 19:6? ("...the dark veil of
unbelief was being cast away from his mind, ...this light
had infused...his soul...the cloud of darkness having
been dispelled...")

IN THE WORLD, BUT NOT OF IT

OBJECTIVE:

To show how we can be free from the world as we rise above it.

EQUIPMENT:

Two glasses of water and a cork.

ACTIVITY AND APPLICATION:

Fill one glass with water up to the brim. Next drop a small cork into the glass of water. Say: I would like to center this cork and make it remain centered. It can't be done. Now add more water until the water rises above the brim and the cork will move to the center. The water and the glass represent the world and the side of the glass represents the evils of the world. When

the cork is centered it represents living in the world, but not of the world. Where is the water in the glass? (It is above the brim.) How are we able to live in the world but not be of the world? (Student choice.) To live in the world of sin we must be able to rise above the world's standards.

IN THE WORLD, BUT NOT OF IT

OBJECTIVE:

To illustrate how a person can live in the world of sin without taking part in it.

EQUIPMENT:

Some large wooden mat-
ches, a glass, a clear
plastic cup with air holes
punched in it, and a glass pie plate ¾ full of water.

ACTIVITY AND APPLICATION:

Set up the following in advance: Attach the end of a match to the inside bottom of the glass and a match to the inside bottom of the plastic cup with the match heads up, see illustration. Now demonstrate the following to the class: Turn the glass and the plastic cup upside down in the pie plate and push them straight down in the water until they touch the bottom of the plate. Lift the glass straight up out of the water, remove the match and strike it. It will light. Ask: Why didn't it get wet? (The air in the glass protected it.) What might the air represent? (The Holy Ghost.) Next lift the plastic cup straight up out of the water, remove the match and strike it. It won't light. Why won't it light? (It's wet.) How did it get wet? (Through the air holes.) What do the air holes in the plastic cup represent? (Evil we let in-to our lives.) What is the effect of evil if we let it come upon us? (It will dampen our spirits.) How can we be in the world, but not of the world? (We can be protected from the evils of the world by the power of the Holy Ghost if we remain faithful and do not become full of the holes caused by sin which causes the Holy Ghost to leave.)

JESUS

OBJECTIVE:

We throw darts at Jesus every time we disobey his commandments.

EQUIPMENT:

A dart and board, a couple of pictures of rough looking people, like a person smoking or drinking, and a picture of Jesus.

ACTIVITY AND APPLICATION:

Hang the dart board in front of the class. Ask a student to come up and try his luck at the bull's eye. Let him practice a couple of times, then ask him to turn around with his back to the dart board. Ask him to follow your instructions exactly as you give them. Instruct him to turn, look and throw. Have him turn around again. Now put up a picture of a rough looking person. Instruct him to turn, look and throw. Repeat this with the second rough looking person. For the last throw, have him turn his back. You will put up the picture of Jesus. This time, instruct him to turn, think and throw. What was different about the last instruction? (Turn, think and throw.) Why? (Student choice.) Ask the student: Why wouldn't you throw at Jesus? Now ask the class: What do you do that is like throwing darts at Jesus? (Student choice.) We throw darts at Jesus every time we disobey his commandments and do not repent.

JOSEPH SMITH

OBJECTIVE:

To show how the Lord was able to take Joseph Smith in his youth and mold him into a great prophet.

EQUIPMENT:

One small tender green willow about three feet long. One large green willow about three feet long.

ACTIVITY AND APPLICATION:

First take the young tender willow and bend it so both ends touch each other. It will not break. Next take the large willow and bend it so both ends touch each other. It will break. Why did one break and the other not? (Student choice.) What are the characteristics of both sticks? (Student choice.) How does this illustration represent Joseph Smith, and why the Lord called him when he was so young. (Student choice.) Joseph Smith was pliable and could be bent and molded in the hands of the Lord to do his will. He was teachable and his mind was not cluttered with the vain traditions of men.

JOSEPH SMITH

OBJECTIVE:

To illustrate that the fruit is no better than the roots.

EQUIPMENT:

A nice shiny apple, and some roots from a tree.

ACTIVITY AND APPLICATION:

Show the apple to the class and make the following statement: I like this apple, but I just can't accept the roots. Show the roots and say: I just can't see how such a small dirty thing like this could produce such a beautiful apple. How is this illustration similar to the following statement made about Joseph Smith? "I admire your church very much, I think I could accept everything about it--except Joseph Smith." If you accept the revelation, what else must you accept? (The revelator.) What do you think the Lord means when he says: "ye shall know them by their fruits"? (Student choice.) "It is a mystery to me how some people speak with admiration for the Church and its work, while at the same time disdaining him through whom, as a servant of the Lord, came the framework of all that the Church is, of all that it stands for. They would pluck the fruit from the tree while cutting off the root from which it grows." (Gordon B. Hinkley conference address April 1977 p. 94).

JUDGING

OBJECTIVE:

To illustrate the positive results of refraining from unrighteous judging or "gossip."

EQUIPMENT:

A large stone, with "The First One" written on it.

ACTIVITY AND APPLICATION:

Place the rock before the class so all can see it. Ask: What do you think is the meaning of this rock? (Student choice.) What did the Lord say about the "First stone"? "He that is without sin let him cast the first stone." Now tell the following story: A very prominent and successful businessman, who still lived a true Christian life, was asked the key to his success. His answer was, "I will show you the key to my success." And taking his friend to the fireplace he showed him there on the mantle, a rock upon which three simple words were painted: "The First One". He said to his friend, "Every morning as I leave for work, I stop just for a moment and look at this stone. It is the first one. As long as I never cast it away, and as long as it is right here, then I know I shall be all right." What can we learn from this story? (Student choice.) Why was the businessman so successful? (Student choice.)

JUDGMENT

OBJECTIVE:

To demonstrate how the Lord's judgments are and will happen.

EQUIPMENT:

A corn grinder, and some corn.

ACTIVITY AND APPLICATION:

Put some corn in the grinder and grind it really fine. Pick some of the cornmeal up and let it run through your fingers. It has been said that the wheels of the Lord grind slowly, but they grind fine. What do you think is meant by that statement? (Student choice.) Why aren't sinners punished immediately? (Student choice.) When will they be punished? (Many continue in their foolish ways, disobeying the living prophet, because they have never been chastized by him. But by and by the Lord's chastening will come as it did to the wicked Nephites. Helaman 10:5-11 and chapter 11.)

KNOWLEDGE

OBJECTIVE:

To illustrate that the value of knowledge lies in our use of it.

EQUIPMENT:

A pocket knife that has two or three blades, and a sharpening stone.

ACTIVITY AND APPLICATION:

Show the knife and the sharpening stone. Show the students how you sharpen the large blade and say: I always sharpen this blade, see how it cuts paper. Cut a piece of paper with the sharp blade. Now show the other blades, they are dull and not used much. What value are these dull blades to me? (Student choice.) How is knowledge and education like my pocket knife? (It's of no value unless we use it.) What is education? (Education is the knowledge of how to use the whole of oneself.) How are men like knives? (Student choice.) Men are often like a knife with many blades. They know how to open them all, but they use only one; all the rest are buried in the handle, and they are no better than they would have been if they had been made with but one blade. Many men use but one or two faculties out of a score with which they are endowed.

LAST DAYS

OBJECTIVE:

To illustrate that no man knoweth the time of the Lord's second coming. Matt. 24:36.

EQUIPMENT:

A wind up clock that works, but it has no hands.

ACTIVITY AND APPLICATION:

Place the clock before the class. Say: Be real quiet and listen to see if you can hear this clock tick. When they hear it, say: Yes it works. This clock represents the topic of todays lesson. What do you think the topic is? (The second coming of Christ.) How does this clock represent the Lord's second coming? (The time is passing, but no one knows what time it is.) No man knows the time of His coming, but how do we know the nearness of the time? (Signs are being fulfilled.) How do you know this clock is getting close to the hour? (You can hear it tick.) How do you know we are getting close to the hour of Christ's coming? (Student choice.)

LIGHT OF THE WORLD

OBJECTIVE:

To demonstrate how we can receive light from the Lord until we become perfect.

EQUIPMENT:

An electric light set up like the one described in the illustration. A quart bottle, a quart of water, and a box of salt.

ACTIVITY AND APPLICATION:

See Matt. 5:13,14, ask: What does the Lord want us to be? (Salt of the earth.) Show a box of salt and ask: What are some of the uses of salt? Savor, preservation, cleanser. So what does the Lord want us to do? (Student choice.) Now demonstrate the following: Put about half an inch of water in the bottle which has previously been placed on the electric light set up, with electric wires in the bottle. Now put just a pinch of salt into the water and stir it until the light comes on. If it doesn't come on the first time add a little more salt. Now ask: If you really are the salt of the earth, what will you become, according to Matt. 5:14? (The light of the world.) See D & C 50:24 and ask: Where do we get light?

(From the Lord.) From the same verse, what happens as we gain more and more light? (We become perfect.) From D&C 93:27-28, how do we receive the fullness? (By keeping the commandments.) What will happen as we continue to keep the commandments? (We will know all things.) In D&C 1:31-33, what does it say will happen to those who sin and repent not? (The light will be taken away.) Now pour more water into the bottle until the light goes out. Now see Matt. 5:13. What did the Lord say would happen when the salt loses its savor? (It is good for nothing.) The Sermon on the Mount is the Lord's blueprint to perfection: if we will live by it we can obtain the Lord's promise of: "Be ye therefore perfect..." Matt. 5:48.

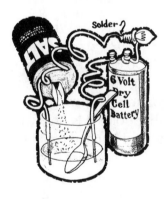

LOVE

OBJECTIVE:

To show how you can tell if a person's love is real.

EQUIPMENT:

An old well-used doll, a nice looking doll with little use.

ACTIVITY AND APPLICATION:

Show the two dolls and ask: Which doll do you think is loved the most? Why? (Student choice.) Now tell the following fable: Two dolls were talking, and one asked the other, "When is it that we dolls become real? Is it when we are wound up, or when we cry or wet?" "Oh, no," said the other doll, "it is only when we have been used and rubbed and hugged so much that we lose our hair, or an eye, and our arms and legs become floppy." Which of these dolls do you think is loved most? (Student choice.) What lesson does this teach about love? (Student choice.) How do you know if a person's love is real? (He takes time, shows interest and he cares.)

MARRIAGE

OBJECTIVE:

To demonstrate how two opposites will not mix.

EQUIPMENT:

A bottle of water with a lid on it, and some motor oil.

ACTIVITY AND APPLICATION:

Demonstrate the following: Here we have some nice clean water and some clean pure oil. How do we get pure clean oil? (Through refining.) How do we get pure clean water? (Distilling it.) Now we will mix some of these two clean pure elements together. Pour some of the oil into the water, replace the lid and shake the bottle. Ask: What's wrong? Why won't they mix? How is this like marriage? (Students choice.) Why won't two people of different religious backgrounds mix, even though they both may be clean and pure? (They are different in standards, beliefs and training.)

65

MARRIAGE

OBJECTIVE:

To show the high value placed on eternal marriage by the Lord.

EQUIPMENT:

An expensive diamond ring and some cheaper jewelry such as: A necklace, bracelet and rings.

ACTIVITY AND APPLICATION:

Show the expensive diamond ring and ask: How much do you think it is worth in dollars? (Student choice.) Tell them the approximate cost. Next show the other jewelry and ask how much they think each is worth. Tell the approximate cost of each. Why did you place such a high price on the diamond ring? (Student choice.) What makes the diamond ring so expensive? Its rarity, hardness, endurance, sparkle and purity. How is an eternal marriage like a diamond ring? (Student choice.) What makes an eternal marriage so valuable? They are for eternity. Purity is a requirement to enter into the temple. They are harder to get and there is a beautiful radiant sparkle about those entering into marriage according to the Lord's way. What makes the diamond ring priceless? (Student choice.) Why is eternal marriage priceless? How does Proverbs 31:10 describe a woman who is a candidate for eternal marriage? ("...a virtuous woman..her, price is far above rubies.)

MISSIONARY WORK

OBJECTIVE:

To demonstrate the Lords challenge of: "...he that thrusteth in his sickle with his might..." D & C 4:4..

EQUIPMENT:

Sickle, long grass or grain.

ACTIVITY AND APPLICATION:

Show the sickle and ask: What is this? How does it work? (Student choice.) What is required to cut grass or grain with a sickle? (A great amount of velocity is required on the part of the person using the sickle.) Demonstrate this as follows: Take the grain and the sickle and just lightly strike the grain with the sickle. Why won't it cut? (Student choice.) What do you think the Lord meant when he said: "...he that thrusteth in his sickle with his might.."? (Student choice.) What will happen if we do our missionary work the way we have to cut grain with the sickle? (Student choice.)

MISSIONARY WORK

OBJECTIVE:

To illustrate the receptive-
ness of some people upon
first hearing the gospel.

EQUIPMENT:

Matches, small wood shavings and a small piece of iron.

ACTIVITY AND APPLICATION:

Light a match and set some wood on fire. Ask: Why
does wood burn? (For years the tree from which the
wood came was absorbing energy from the sunlight and
storing it in the form of hydro-carbons, (hydrogen and
carbon). Whenever a spark of fire comes in contact with
the wood, it immediately releases the energy that it has
stored within itself.) Now light another match and set it
to a piece of iron and ask: Why doesn't the iron burn?
(Iron will not burn by its own energy because it has
none; it will only burn as a result of extreme amounts of
heat supplied from another source.) How are men like
wood? (Student choice.) How do people respond to a
spark? (Once they take fire, the spirit within them eager-
ly seeks release in the form of enthusiastic activity in the
church.) What must a person have before they can start
a flame in someone else's heart? (They must have a fire
burning within their own heart.) Some people are very
receptive to the gospel because they have been storing
up spiritual energy for years. How are some people like
iron? (Student choice.)

MISSIONARY WORK

OBJECTIVE:

To demonstrate how many people are attracted to the gospel when the right power is used.

EQUIPMENT:

A small bottle of sand, dirt and iron filings. A small magnet.

ACTIVITY AND APPLICATION:

Show the bottle of elements to each of the class members and ask them to identify something in the bottle. Next take the magnet and sweep it through the bottle, and show how it draws something good out of all the trash. Ask: Why are the iron filings attracted? (Student choice.) What does this teach us about doing missionary work? (There are many honest in heart mixed in the world with all the rest.) What does it take to separate the honest in heart from the rest? (The right power of attraction through the power of the Holy Ghost.) Why are some attracted while others are not? (Some are the right material, they are receptive to the spirit and will be gathered into the house of Israel. Others do not have what it takes to be attracted.)

MORALITY

OBJECTIVE:

To demonstrate how Satan and evil cannot harm you as long as you are clean and pure.

EQUIPMENT:

Two sugar cubes, matches, tweezers and cigarette ashes in a bottle.

ACTIVITY AND APPLICATION:

Show a pure white sugar cube and a match and explain: My objective will be to light this sugar cube. Turn off the class lights and light a match and hold it to the sugar cube. It will not burn. Next put another sugar cube inside the bottle with the cigarette ashes and shake it a little. Pull the sugar cube out with the tweezers and try to set fire to it. It will burn. Why does this one burn while the first one would not? The impurities on it make it combustible. How is this like moral cleanliness? (Student choice.) When is the only time Satan can harm us? (Satan does not have the power to harm us unless we submit to his lusts and evil designs.) According to James 1:14 what causes temptation? ("...But every man is tempted, when he is drawn away of his own lust, and enticed."

70

MORALITY

OBJECTIVE:

To demonstrate the seriousness of losing one's chastity.

EQUIPMENT:

A package of "sweet and juicy" gum, soap and warm water and paper towels.

ACTIVITY AND APPLICATION:

Show the class the package of gum and ask, "Who would like some of this nice juicy gum?" Before you give it to him unwrap it and chew it until all the sweet juice is out of it. Next take the gum out and throw it on the floor or ground and stomp on it. Now offer it to the student. Say: "Oh, it needs to be cleaned first." Wash it with the soap and water, square it up and wrap it up again. Now offer it to the student. How is this like being morally clean? (Student choice.) When it comes to selecting a mate, who would you like? (Student choice.) No one wants one that has been passed around in filth. Why can't we expect to wallow in filth and be able to return to our original virtuous state, without a lot of hard work and repentance? (Now if there is true repentance, the Lord in some miraculous way will change it for a brand new piece.) Now give the student a nice new piece of gum.

MORAL PURITY

OBJECTIVE:

To illustrate how we must take the prescriptions given to us by our spiritual leaders, teachers and parents in order to cure us of the ills which exist in the world today.

EQUIPMENT:

A medicine bottle.

ACTIVITY AND APPLICATION:

Show the medicine bottle and relate the following: A recent survey in a large medical center showed a very large number of illnesses had been diagnosed and prescriptions given to treat the illness, but the prescriptions had never been filled. How does this same principle apply to the spiritual illnesses in the world today? (Student choice.) Why do you think a person would get a prescription from a doctor, but never use the medicine? (Student choice.) What medicine do you think should be taken daily in order to avoid the spiritual sicknesses of our time? (Daily prayer, scripture study and meditation.) Why do you think some people refuse to take the medicine that has been prescribed by our spiritual leaders? (Student choice.)

NATURAL MAN

OBJECTIVE:

To demonstrate that the natural eye cannot always see things as they are.

EQUIPMENT:

Binoculars, regular glasses and a stake with the word "Obey" written on it.

ACTIVITY AND APPLICATION:

Prior to class place the stake outside at a distance far enough away so that the word "obey" can't be read with the natural eye but can be read with the binoculars. Tell the class that you have a stake outside with some instructions written on it. Ask a student to read it with his natural eye. He won't be able to see it. Ask; "Why can't you read it?" Now give him some regular glasses and have him try to read it. Ask; "Why don't the glasses help?" Now give him the binoculars and ask him to read what it says on the stake. "Why can he read it now?" (Student choice.) "Why can't we always see things the way the Lord wants us to?" "According to Mosiah 3:19, how are we able to see things God's way?" ("...the natural man is an enemy to God.." In order for us to see the things that we should do and obey them, we must put on our spiritual glasses and see things as the Lord sees them.)

OATH

OBJECTIVE:

To illustrate how an oath must be kept firm and strong.

EQUIPMENT:

A pan of water.

ACTIVITY AND APPLICATION:

Ask: What is an oath? (Student choice.) Demonstrate how you can hold water in your cupped hand. What happens if the hands are not kept tight? Show how the water goes through the fingers. How is this illustration like an oath? (Student choice.) Tell the following story from Sir Thomas More in the movie "A Man for all Seasons." Sir Thomas More understood the power of promises. He wouldn't take an oath to support Henry VIII's divorce, and because of it he lost everything. When he was imprisoned in the tower London, his daughter came to him saying that the family has no more provisions, and sits in silence, wondering what will happen to him. "Father", she says, "God more regards the thoughts of the heart than the words of the mouth, or so you've always told me." More, "Yes." Margaret, "Then say the words of the oath and in your heart think otherwise." Ask: Why can't you do that? (Student choice.) Continue the story: "What is an oath then but words we say to God? Listen, Meg. When a man takes an oath, he's holding his own self in his own hands. And if he opens his fingers, then he needn't hope to find himself again." Why is it impossible to do or say something and in your heart think otherwise? (Student choice.) How is an oath like water in your hands? (Student choice.)

OBEDIENCE

OBJECTIVE:

To illustrate the danger of ignoring the counsel of our
leaders.

EQUIPMENT:

A mouse trap and a rubber mouse.

ACTIVITY AND APPLICATION:

Show the mouse trap and the mouse in the ap-
propriate place as you quote the following poem: First
show the mouse trap.

    "Once there was a mouse trap
      baited with some cheese;
    It tickled so the little mouse (show the little mouse)
      it almost made him sneeze;
    An older mouse said,
      "There's danger, be careful where you go."
    "Nonsense", said the little mouse,
    "I don't think you know."
    So he went in boldly, (move the mouse in next
      to the trap) no one was in sight,
    First he took a nibble, (let mouse nibble side
      of trap) then he took a bite.
    (Put the mouse's nose on the trigger of the trap.)
    And snap went the clapper as quickly as a wink, and
      caught the little mouse, because he didn't think!"
    Author unknown

What is a lesson on obedience? (Student choice.) What

was the little mouse's first mistake? (Ignoring the advice of his elder.) What is the value of listening to those who are older? (Student choice.) How does Satan work? (He gets us to take a little nibble at first and then we take a bite and then he catches us.)

OBEDIENCE

OBJECTIVE:

To illustrate how faithless and simple disobedient the children of Israel were, and how many are the same way today.

EQUIPMENT:

A rubber play snake attached to a wooden pole.

ACTIVITY AND APPLICATION:

Show the snake on the pole as you tell the story found in Numbers 21:8, 9. What simple act of faith was required? Just look upon the snake. That was a simple enough request. Why do you think it was so hard for many to do it? (Student choice.) What simple requests has the Lord given us today which contain promises to those who will do them? (Student choice.) What are the promises of the following principles we have been asked to live:

1. The payment of tithing--The Lord will open the windows of heaven.

2. Living the Word of Wisdom--Greater health.

3. Family home evening--Your children will not go astray

4. Reading the Scriptures--Bring you closer to Heavenly Father.

5. Being morally clean--Eternal marriage.

6. Raising a garden and food storage--Physical preparedness.

The above list is only a few of the many things we have been asked to do, but still some say I will not do it. Why is the act of obedience more important than any of the benefits? (Student choice.)

OPPOSITION

OBJECTIVE:

To illustrate the different reactions to life's trials, obstacles and opposition.

EQUIPMENT:

A hand grindstone, some soft wood, chalk, knife and polished rock.

ACTIVITY AND APPLICATION:

Turn the handle on the grindstone and say: It has been said that life is a grindstone, and whether it grinds you down, (grind the wood or chalk) or polishes you up, (show the polished rock) or sharpens you up (sharpen the knife) all depends on what? (What you are made of.) In life who gets ground down? Who gets polished up? (Student choice.) It's like the coach who sends his squad through grueling practices and brings out an organized machine that works like a clock. If you have the right quality, you will take polish and sharpening. If you don't you will be ground down under the pressure.

PERSONALITY

OBJECTIVE:

To illustrate the miracle of personality.

EQUIPMENT:

Two black walnuts, one whole and one split in half.

ACTIVITY AND APPLICATION:

Show the whole black walnut and explain: I hold in my hand a black walnut. (Put it on the floor and stand on it.) What are its qualities? (Student choice.) (It has a shell like a stone.) Show the split walnut and ask: Why is it so strong? (It has many internal reinforcements.) What is the potential of the walnut? In between the reinforcements is an unimpressive, unimportant looking meaty substance that has a mysterious and tremendous power. If you plant this seed under certain circumstances, heat is produced inside. This walnut then produces a mysterious power that breaks the stony shell as though it were paper, and a little shoot works its way up through the soil to become a great walnut tree. What is it that breaks

the hard tough walnut shell? (Some miraculous power.) Every human being has inside him a far greater power; a power to influence others. What do you think this power is? Personality. What does it take to break a person's personality open so that he blesses others? The greatest of all the miracles is the miracle of personality. It has been said that 85 percent of all of your success in life depends on your personality.

POTENTIAL

OBJECTIVE:

Show why all the students have the same potential for growth in this class.

EQUIPMENT:

Two peaches, one very large, one very small; and a peach seed.

ACTIVITY AND APPLICATION:

Show the peach seed and ask: What is its potential? (Student choice.) Why can this seed become a peach tree and produce peaches? (It is the offspring of a peach.) Now show the two peaches, the large one and the small one together, and explain: These two peaches came off the same tree. Why is there so much difference in their size? (The one received more light and nourishment from the sun.) Why? Where do you think the big peach was located on the tree? (Up high.) Now the peach had no choice where it was located on the tree, but why is that not true with you? How does this seed represent your potential in this class? You all have the same equal chance to grow from this class. How is your growth in this class like the peaches? (Student choice.) What will determine what you become as a result of this class? (It will depend upon what you take advantage of.) Why will some receive more nourishment and light than others? (Student choice.)

POTENTIAL

OBJECTIVE:

To demonstrate the unlimited nature of our potential.

EQUIPMENT:

A large watermelon and a watermelon seed.

ACTIVITY AND APPLICATION:

Show the watermelon seed and ask: What is this? What is its potential? (Student choice.) Next show the watermelon and explain: This watermelon has the power of drawing from the ground through itself 200,000 times it weight, in 90 days. That's not all; it blends beautiful color and design, and best of all a wonderful delicious taste. All this from one little black seed. How is your potential like the watermelon? (Student choice.) How are we able to become 200,000 times better? (Student choice.) We too have a great potential; as a child of God our potential is "...to become perfect even as our Father which is in Heaven is perfect."

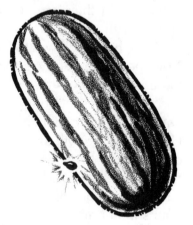

PRIDE

OBJECTIVE:

To demonstrate why anyone can be replaced.

EQUIPMENT:

A gallon bottle about three fourths full of water.

ACTIVITY AND APPLICATION:

Show the bottle of water and recite the following poem:

"Sometime, when you're feeling important.
Sometime when your ego's in bloom.
 Sometime when you take it for granted
   you're the most qualified in the room.
Sometime when you feel that your going would
   leave an unfillable hole,
Just try this simple instruction
   and see how it humbles your soul.
Take a bottle and fill it with water,
   Put your hand in it up to the wrist;
(put your hand in it up to the wrist) Pull it out,
   (pull your hand out) and the hole that's
   remaining is a measure of how you'll be missed.
You may splash all you want when you enter,
   You may stir up the water galore,
But stop, and you'll find in a moment

that it looks quite the same as before.
What is the moral of this illustration?
   (Student choice.)
The moral of this quaint example
   is to do just the best that you can
be proud of yourself-but remember
   THERE IS NO INDISPENSABLE MAN!
Why is there no indispensable man? Author unknown.
In the Lord's Church there is always someone who can
take over any position at any time. The Lord makes us
equal to the task when we accept our assignment with
humility.

PROCRASTINATION

OBJECTIVE:

To illustrate the folly of putting off repentance.

EQUIPMENT:

Half of a pair of pliers.

ACTIVITY AND APPLICATION:

Show the pliers and tell the following story: Sometime ago I noticed that the nut on these pliers was loose. I intended on tightening it right then, but as you see I didn't, and now it's too late; the other half is lost. How is this situation like failure to repent? (Student choice.) When is the best time to fix the pliers? (When you notice they are loose.) When is the best time to repent? (When you notice you are loose in your thoughts and actions.) What are some loose habits in our day? (Student choice.) In Alma 34:32-35, what does Amulek say about repentance? "...I beseech of you that ye do not procrastinate the day of your repentance until the end...then cometh the night of darkness wherein there can be no labor performed."

PROTECTIVE COATING

OBJECTIVE:

To show how a protective coating keeps us from being hurt by the fires of Satan.

EQUIPMENT:

Rubbing alcohol, matches and some Q-tips.

ACTIVITY AND APPLICATION:

Show the first Q-tip and light a match to it. It will burn and turn black. Dip the second Q-tip into the alcohol and light a match to it. Blow the fire out before it burns up all the alcohol. Show it to the class and ask: Why didn't it burn? Why did the first one burn? (Student choice.) What are some good protective coatings we can have to protect us from being burned by evil? (Student choice.) Even though the fiery darts of the evil one are constantly around us, we will not be burned by him as long as we keep a good protective coating of moral purity, chastity, and keeping the commandments.

PURITY

OBJECTIVE:

To show how we can re-main clean and pure if we keep the spirit of the Lord inside us.

EQUIPMENT:

A pint jar, a glass pie plate, a rubber hose and some food coloring.

ACTIVITY AND APPLICATION:

Fill the pie plate half full of colored water. Stand the jar upside down in the pie plate. Push one end of the rub-ber hose inside the jar until the end touches the bottom of the bottle. Put the other end of the hose in your mouth and suck the air out of the bottle. The water will begin to rise in the bottle. Continue sucking the air out until the water reaches the top of the hose, the water should remain in the bottle without escaping. Now the air represents the spirit of the Lord, and the colored water represents evil. Why did the water enter? (The air went out.) How does evil get in? (The spirit goes out.) It is a natural law that both air and water cannot occupy the same space. How does this same law exist with us? (Student choice.)

PURITY

OBJECTIVE:

To demonstrate the Lord's statement: "Neither do men put new wine into old bottles:..." Matt. 9:17.

EQUIPMENT:

A very dirty vessel, some fresh clean drinking water.

ACTIVITY AND APPLICATION:

Show a pure glass of clean fresh drinking water and ask: How do you like your water? What are some uses of water? (Student choice.) Drink some of the clean water. Now pour the water into the very dirty vessel. Now what are its uses? (Student choice.) What does the following statement of the Savior mean to you? "Unless the vessel is clean, whatever you pour into it turns sour?" (Student choice.) Why must our inner vessel be clean in order for virtuous experiences to have any wholesome effect upon us? (Student choice.)

REBELLION

OBJECTIVE:

To illustrate why it is hard to kick against the pricks, Acts 9:5.

EQUIPMENT:

Some part of a horse harness, such as: The collar and hames.

ACTIVITY AND APPLICATION:

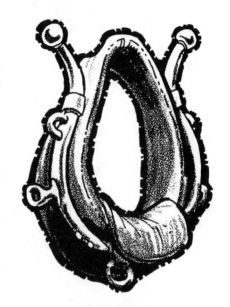

Hold the collar and hames before the class and ask: What are these? What are they used for? What is required when you have two horses harnessed together pulling a load? (Student choice.) What would happen if two horses were hooked to a wagon and one spent all his time kicking and balking? (Student choice.) Now quote the following poem:

"A horse can't pull while kicking.
   This fact I merely mention.
And he can't kick while pulling,
   which is my chief contention.
So let's imitate the good old horse
   and lead a life that's fitting.
Just pull an honest load and
   then there'll be no time for kicking."
   Author unknown

What is the moral of this poem? (Student choice.) How are people like horses? As long as one person in the team is kicking no one makes any progress. If we all pull our share of the load to accomplish the task, then all are rewarded.

REPENTANCE

OBJECTIVE:

To show how sins, though "They be as scarlet, they shall be as white as snow." Isaiah 1:18.

EQUIPMENT:

A small bottle half full of water and three bottles with the following special chemicals in them. The first bottle has Phenolphthalein and is labeled "Temptation". The second has Sodium Hydroxide (Liquid Drano) and is labeled "Sin". The third has Hydrochloric acid (Liquid Lye) and is labeled "Repentance".

ACTIVITY AND APPLICATION:

Show the three labeled bottles. Take the small bottle of water and drop into it a few drops from the temptation bottle. Ask: Why is there temptation? (Student choice.) Now add a few drops from the sin bottle, and the contents will turn red. Refer to Isaiah 1:18. "From this scripture, what does Isaiah say can happen even though your sins be as scarlet?" Drop in a few drops from the repentance bottle. According to the demonstration what happens when we repent? (Student choice.) What was required to change the water from scarlet red to clear water? (The proper chemical.) What is required in order to be cleansed from our sins? (When repentance contains the proper ingredient our sins will be completely washed away.) What are the proper steps in repentance? (Realize the sin, feel sorry, stop the sin, confession, make restitution and replace the sin with good work.)

REPENTANCE

OBJECTIVE:

To demonstrate how the cleansing must take place within.

EQUIPMENT:

Two dirty bottles, one with a lid on it. Smear mud on the inside and outside of both bottles. Some warm soapy water and some clean rinse water.

ACTIVITY AND APPLICATION:

First take the bottle with the lid on it, show it to the class and say: See, this bottle is really dirty. Put it in the soapy water and wash it and then rinse it and wipe it dry. Show it to the class and ask: Why isn't it clean? (Student choice.) Now show the second bottle, the one without a lid. See it is very dirty, but I'm only going to wash the inside, that is my main goal, just the inside. Put it in the soapy water and scrub the inside very thoroughly, then rinse and wipe the inside dry with a paper towel. What hap-pened? (Student choice.) According to Alma 60:23, what happened? "...the inward vessel shall be cleansed first, and then shall the outer vessel be cleansed also.

REPENTANCE

OBJECTIVE:

To demonstrate how repentance must be proper and complete in order to be effective.

EQUIPMENT:

A bar of soap, some dish detergent, a scrub brush, a pan of hot water, some paper towels, and a pair of black greasy hands. (Put black grease on your hands)

ACTIVITY AND APPLICATION:

Show your hands and offer to shake hands with anyone. Show the bar of soap and ask: Why is repentance called the soap of life? (Student choice.) Let me demonstrate. First wash your hands in the water only. Show your hands and ask: How does this represent how repentance is often used? (Student choice.) Next wash your hands again using just a little hand soap. Show your hands again. Why aren't they clean, I used soap? (Student choice.) Last, wash again using lots of soap, both hand and dish detergent, along with the scrub brush. Now, what was required to get my hands clean of the filth? (Student choice.) How is this like repentance? (Student choice.) Repentance is a beautiful cleansing process which takes a lot of hard work and the proper steps.

RESISTING TEMPTATION

OBJECTIVE:

To demonstrate why it's so hard for some people to resist temptation and sin.

EQUIPMENT:

Two sugar cubes, some powdered sugar, some red food coloring, a glass pie plate and a little water.

ACTIVITY AND APPLICATION:

Put two or three tablespoons of colored water in the center of the pie plate. Stack the two sugar cubes on each other with powdered sugar heaped on the top sugar cube. Place the stack of sugar in the colored water. Watch the water rise up through the sugar cubes. Ask: Why does the water go through the sugar cubes and not the powdered sugar? (The sugar cubes are porous or full of holes and are unable to resist the water, but the powdered sugar is smooth and refined and has no air spaces and is able to resist the influence of the water longer.) The sugar represents people and the colored water represents sin or evil. How are people like sugar cubes and powdered sugar? (Student choice.) Why are some people more resistant to temptation and sin than others? (Student choice.) A person whose testimony and standards are full of holes is an easy victim for the devil. But the person who is pure and refined and free of loop holes can resist the devil.

RESISTING TEMPTATION

OBJECTIVE:

To show how to resist the
devil. James 4:7 Submit
yourselves... to God.
Resist the devil, and he
will flee from you.

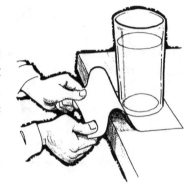

EQUIPMENT:

A glass full of water and a sheet of regular type paper.

ACTIVITY AND APPLICATION:

Lay a sheet of type paper flat on a bare table, set the
glass of water on the type paper about two inches from
the top end of the paper. Now with both hands, take
hold of the paper and pull it slowly toward you. The
glass will move along with the paper. Now put the
paper and glass back in their original position. Take
hold of the bottom of the paper with both hands and
push the lower edge toward the glass until there is a big
bend in the paper between your hands and the glass.
Then, keeping your hands close to the top of the table,
jerk the paper toward you quickly. The paper will
come out from under the glass, leaving the glass standing where it was. What can we learn about getting
away from evil from this illustration (Student choice.)
What is the best way to get rid of evil temptation? (Student choice.) From the scripture in James 4:7, how do
we get away from evil temptation? (Flee from it
quickly.)

SABBATH

OBJECTIVE:

To illustrate the importance of the Lord's day.

EQUIPMENT:

Seven cookies on a plate.

ACTIVITY AND APPLICATION:

In advance prepare a student to demonstrate the following with you: Tell him that you will give him six of the seven cookies on the plate, but when I turn my back to write on the chalk board, he is to take the seventh also, and return to his seat. In starting the presentation, tell the class that you have six cookies you would like to give to ___STUDENT'S NAME___, because he is such a nice guy. Call the student up and say: You can have these six cookies, they are yours and you can do anything you want with them. Now turn your back to the student to write on the board. Write: Are you honest? When you turn your back the student will take the seventh cookie also. When you turn back around and notice the seventh cookie is gone, ask: Ok who took the other one? When you find out, go to the student with the cookies and take them all away from him. What topic do you think this represents? (The Sabbath day.) How is our

illustration like the Sabbath day? (Student choice.) What do you think of a person who would be given six cookies and then steal the seventh? (Student choice.) The Lord gives us six days a week to do all our work, play, recreation, and pleasures. He keeps the seventh, it is His. But while He is not looking (so they think) many steal the seventh also. How are the results of breaking the Sabbath day like taking all the cookies away from the student? (When we break this commandment of the Lord's, He takes all the blessings away from us.)

SATAN'S LURES

OBJECTIVE:

To illustrate how Satan uses lures to catch people in the same manner people use lures to catch fish.

EQUIPMENT:

Two complete fishing poles, complete with reel and line. Attach lures and bait to one, and attach a string with cigarette, alcohol and beer containers to the other.

ACTIVITY AND APPLICATION:

First dangle the pole with the lures in front of the students and ask: What is the gear on this pole called? (Lures.) Why? (Student choice.) What are the characteristics of fish lures? (They're bright, shiny and attractive.) How does it work? (Student choice.) Now show the other fishing pole and ask: How are these things similar to those on the first pole? (Student choice.) Who uses these lures? Satan. How does he use them? Why? Satan uses lures; he uses the most colorful and attractive ones thought of. Many people, especially young people are attracted by these. Once they get close to them, what usually happens? (They get caught.)

SCATTERING OF ISRAEL

OBJECTIVE:

To illustrate how the scattering of Israel was an act of salting the earth. Matt. 5:13,14 and Gen. 12:3.

EQUIPMENT:

Globe map and a large box of salt.

ACTIVITY AND APPLICATION:

Tell the students that the following demonstration will give them a clue as to why the Lord caused Israel to be scattered. Sprinkle some salt on the globe map, and ask: What does Matt. 5:13 say about salt? ("ye are the salt of the earth.") From Gen. 12:3, how did you become the salt of the earth? (All nations of the earth have been blessed because of the scattering of Israel.)

SCRIPTURES

OBJECTIVE:

To illustrate how comfortable the scriptures should become for us.

EQUIPMENT:

A pair of well worn tennis shoes, a pair of brand new tennis shoes and two sets of scriptures, one well used and the other brand new.

ACTIVITY AND APPLICATION:

Present the following situation: Let's assume that you were going to participate in a championship event-- basketball, or tennis or cross country track. These are both your shoes; and you have your choice. Which would you choose? Show the well used pair and say: See, these are all scuffed up and not shiny or new. Next show the new pair and say: See, these are brand new, never been used. Now which pair would you choose? Why? Now show the two sets of scriptures, the new and the old well used. If these were your scriptures and you were going to have a scripture discussion with someone, which ones would you use? Why? (Student choice.) "Let these scriptures become worn and used so they will feel as comfortable in your hands as well-worn tennis shoes do on your feet." J. Thomas Fyans conference report April 77 p.54.

SCRIPTURES

OBJECTIVE:

To demonstrate how we can accomplish a hard task, such as reading the Bible, by constant continued effort, rather than all at once.

EQUIPMENT:

A Bible or other scriptures and some string.

ACTIVITY AND APPLICATION:

Tie some heavy string around the book of scripture, lengthwise. Attach a lighter string to the heavy string at the top and the bottom, about three feet long each. Suspend the book to a hook in the ceiling with the top string. The other string will hang below the book. Now demonstrate the following: My purpose is to pull on this bottom string and cause the book to fall down. Be ready to catch the book. On the first attempt, grab the string and give it a quick jerk. The string will break leaving the book suspended. Tie the string back on the bottom of the book. Now pull on the string hard and steady until the string breaks. It will break at the upper end and the book will fall. From this illustration how is the best way to read the scriptures? (Student choice.) Why can you read the scriptures best if you do it steadily every day? (Student choice.) It becomes a habit and we accomplish more by steady, consistent effort than by quick, hasty hits and misses.

SCRIPTURES

OBJECTIVE:

It takes more than just reading to get excited about the scriptures.

EQUIPMENT:

Two glasses ⅓ full of water, some soda, vinegar and a spoon.

ACTIVITY AND APPLICATION:

Explain that these two glasses represent two students who have their scriptures. Now add a teaspoon full of soda to both glasses. This represents reading the scriptures, both students have read the scriptures. Now one of the students has done something in addition to reading. Add the vinegar to one glass until the water runs over the top. What do you think the vinegar represents that the student did in addition to reading? (Student choice.) When we study, search and pray about the scriptures as we read them, we become enthusiastic about them and overflow with the spirit.

SEEK YE FIRST...

OBJECTIVE:

To illustrate the Lords statement: "But seek ye first the kingdom of God, and his righteousness; and all these things shall be added unto you. Matt. 6:33.

EQUIPMENT:

Three glass bottles, equal size, one full of smooth shiny rocks and labeled "Gospel principles", one about ¾ full of salt and labeled "Riches", and one empty and labeled "Our life".

ACTIVITY AND APPLICATION:

Make sure that the rocks and salt are the correct amount to fill the empty bottle when the rocks are added first and then the salt is added and shaken in. Demonstrate the following: Pour the salt into the bottle labeled "Our life" explaining that we want you to have the joy of life's riches. Why does the Lord want you to have material riches? (Student choice.) Now we also want you to have the great blessings of all the beautiful gospel truths. Show the rocks one at a time labeling them by gospel principles such as: Faith, repentance, tithing, Word of Wisdom, temple marriage, family, testimony, etc. Now add the rocks to the bottle labeled "Our life" along with the salt. You will get only a few of the rocks into the bottle. Remove the rocks and the salt and put them back into their original bottles. Now demonstrate the same illustration again, but this time add the rocks to the bottle labeled "Our life" first. Add the salt, shaking it so that you get all of the salt in. What were we able to do this time that we didn't do the first time? Why? (Student choice.) What must we do to be able to have both the gospel truths and the material riches? (Student choice.) What does the Lord mean when he says: "...Seek ye first the kingdom of God,...and all these things shall be added unto you? (Student choice.)

SIN

OBJECTIVE:

To illustrate the danger of little, so-called, insignificant sins.

EQUIPMENT:

Two clocks.

ACTIVITY AND APPLICATION:

Show the two clocks as follows: The first one will be set close to the correct time, just five minutes off. The second one will be set five hours off the correct time. Ask: Which clock is the most misleading? Why? (Student choice.) How are sins like these two clocks? (Student choice.) Which sins are most misleading? (The small ones.) Why? (Student choice.) Big terrible sins are readily noticeable to the person with common sense. The big sins have very little influence or temptation. But the little innocent sins, the hard to recognize sins, are the ones that catch us and burden us down.

SIN

OBJECTIVE:

To demonstrate how little sins get the best of us.

EQUIPMENT:

A glass nearly filled to the brim with water and about 30 coins--pennies, nickles, dimes and quarters.

ACTIVITY AND APPLICATION:

Fill the glass nearly to the brim with water. Show the coins and ask: How many coins do you think we can put into the glass of water before the water runs over the top? (Student choice.) These coins represent individual sins. Now begin putting the coins into the glass of water, starting first with the small coins and then the larger ones. Ask: How is sinning like this illustration? (Student choice.) What does one sin lead to? Why? (Student choice.) Now continue putting the coins into the glass of water until it finally runs over the top. Say: No one in the class knew the breaking point of the water. How is this like sin? There is a point in which little sins will break us. We don't know when that is so we must break the sin habit before they break us.

SIN

OBJECTIVE:

To demonstrate what happens when we tamper with sin.

EQUIPMENT:

A powerful horseshoe magnet, many straight pins and an overhead projector.

ACTIVITY AND APPLICATION:

Spread the pins out on the overhead projector. Now with the magnet, see how close you can get to the pins, trying not to attract any. Why is it so hard to resist attracting any of the pins to the magnet? (Student choice.) The magnet represents the power of the evil one and the pins represent little sins. What causes us to commit little sins? (Student choice.) Why is it so hard to resist Satan's temptations when we go upon his playground? (Student choice.) Now pull off the few pins that are on the magnet, showing how easy it is to get just a few off. Grab all the pins with the magnet and challenge someone to pull them all off at once. It can't be done. How is this illustration like sins? (Student choice.) When is the best time to get rid of sins? (Student choice.) What happens if we let many little sins pile up without getting rid of them? (Student choice.)

SIN

OBJECTIVE:

To illustrate the folly of the following statement: "It's nobody's business what I do; I only hurt myself."

EQUIPMENT:

Three boards connected together with a bolt as illustrated. Label the top board "Self", middle board "Loved Ones", and bottom board "Lord"; a large nail and a hammer.

ACTIVITY AND APPLICATION:

Show the boards connected together with the top board "Self" showing. Make the following statement: When I do something wrong it's nobody's business but my own. Now hammer the nail through all three boards. Show the boards just like you did at first and ask: What's wrong with the statement I made? (Student choice.) Now pull out the nail and ask: Who else is hurt? Spread out the other two boards as illustrated and ask: How are loved ones hurt? (Student choice.) Why does it hurt the Lord? (Student choice.) Why is the following state- ment true: Everything we do in this life affects someone else, ourselves, loved ones which includes friends and the Lord? (Student choice.)

SOCIAL PRESSURE

OBJECTIVE:

To show how Satan's decoys lead us to danger.

EQUIPMENT:

A real goose decoy, a goose call and some pictures of evil ads of alcohol and tobacco.

ACTIVITY AND APPLICATION:

Show the goose decoy, and make the sound of a goose, using the goose call. Ask: What is the true meaning of decoy? (To allure into danger..even to death.) What happens when these two objects are used by a skillful hunter? (Live geese are attracted.) Why are geese attracted by them? In the mind of a true sportsman a decoy is an imitation goose placed in the water to lure other geese into the area. Geese are like humans; they like companionship and when they see the decoys in the water, they swoop down to land beside them. What will most likely happen if the geese are lured to the decoys? (Danger or destruction.) How does Satan use decoys? (Student choice.) What are some of Satan's decoys? (Student choice.) How is Satan like the hunter? The hunter is waiting with his gun to kill the geese as they come within range; likewise Satan uses some very attractive lures in evil advertisements, filthy movies and literature to attract people into danger. His intention is to kill us spiritually as well as physically.

SPIRITUAL ACTIVITY

OBJECTIVE:

To demonstrate how we must receive spiritual power and direction to keep going.

EQUIPMENT:

A special top called "Top Secret" made by Andrews Mf Co. Eugene, Oregon 97403.

ACTIVITY AND APPLICATION:

First show the little top. Spin the top on a table top where all can see. Watch what happens. The top will either stop after a while or spin off the table. Now spin the top in the base provided with the top. It will spin continuously, never stopping, and will remain on course. Ask: What happened to the first top? Why? (Student choice.) What happened the second time that was different from the first? (It didn't stop and it remained on course.) Why does it keep going? (I can't tell you, it's "top secret".) The base has something built in it that gives the top energy. Why does it remain on course? (The base gives it direction and confinement.) How is the gospel like the base of this top? (Student choice.) The source of power and direction for our lives is the gospel of Jesus Christ. As long as we remain within its influence we will receive power to keep going and will always remain on course.

SPIRITUALITY

OBJECTIVE:

To demonstrate the effect of one's spiritual sharpness.

EQUIPMENT:

A brace and bit; two drill bits, one old and rusted with the threads worn off the end; and one in good condition with good threads and a block of wood.

ACTIVITY AND APPLICATION:

Demonstrate how the good bit drills, going very deep with very little effort. How does this represent a spiritually sharp person? (Student choice.) Next demonstrate the old bit. See how it turns and turns, but makes no depth. Why won't this one drill? (Student choice.) When our spiritual threads are sharp we will have greater depth in the gospel; our roots will run deep. If our spiritual threads are worn out or become dull, we will just go through the motions without gaining any depth.

SPIRITUAL MATURITY

OBJECTIVE:

To demonstrate the dif-
ference between a
spiritually weak person
and a spiritually mature
person.

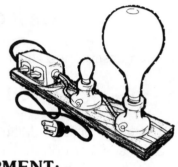

EQUIPMENT:

Two electric light bulbs in sockets, one 10 watt bulb
and one 1500 watt bulb.

ACTIVITY AND APPLICATION:

Draw the students attention to the two lights that are
sitting on the table in front of them. Tell them to watch
everything that happens. Now do the following in this
order: 1. Turn off all the class lights. 2. Turn on the 10
watt bulb. 3. Turn on the 1500 watt bulb. 4. Turn off
the 10 watt bulb. 5. Turn off the 1500 watt bulb. Do all
this without saying anything. Turn the class lights on
again. After you've completed the five steps ask the
students to tell anything about what they observed.
(Student choice.) How would you liken the two lights
to two people? (Student choice.) The small light made
little or no difference. How is this like some people?
(Some people radiate greater light and influence upon
others.) What happened when the small light was turned off? (It wasn't missed, and it went out immediately.)
How is this like a person who is spiritually small? (Student choice.) What happened when the large light was

turned off? (It's light faded out slowly.) How is this like a spiritually mature person? (He does not lose the spirit easily, and when he is tested he is able to endure. How many volts are both sockets wired for? (The same.) How is our spiritual potential like the voltage to a light socket? (The Lord wired us all with the same spiritual capacity, but many are not using their spiritual potential.)

STANDARDS

OBJECTIVE:

To illustrate how the gospel standards are straight and undeviating.

EQUIPMENT:

Four cardboard cards, four inches square, with a one inch square cut in the center of each; four wooden bases, with a slit cut across the middle of each; a three foot 2x4 and a candle.

ACTIVITY AND APPLICATION:

Place the four cards in the slits of the four wooden bases and line them up one behind the other in a straight line along the 2x4 about a foot apart. Stand the candle directly behind the hole of the last card and light it. Move the board around so all can see. Ask: What do you see as you look through the holes in the cards? Now move one or two of the blocks to the left or right just a little. You will not be able to see the light. Ask. Why can't you see the light now? How does light travel? (In a straight line.) How is the gospel like light? (Student choice.) Just as light travels in a straight line, the standards of the gospel are straight and undeviating. What happens when we are out of line just a little with any of the principles of the gospel? (We lose the light.) What must we do in order to see the light again? (We must get back into line again.)

SUCCESS

OBJECTIVE:

To demonstrate how the person large in spirit and work always rises above the small.

EQUIPMENT:

A quart bottle over ½ full of beans and one walnut.

ACTIVITY AND APPLICATION:

Show the bottle of beans with the walnut in the bottle on top of the beans. Demonstrate and explain that even if we turn the bottle over and put the walnut on the bottom, the walnut will always come to the top. Now shake the bottle and the walnut will rise to the top. Repeat this again explaining that you just can't keep it down. What makes the walnut rise to the top? (Student choice.) It has been said that you just can't keep a good man who is willing to work down. What does this mean? (Student choice.) The large in spirit and work will always rise to the top. So what is it that separates the large from the small? (Student choice.)

TALENTS

OBJECTIVE:

To demonstrate how some people get their talent dampened by others before they even start.

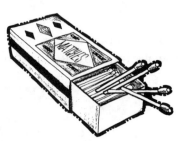

EQUIPMENT:

Matches, some good dry matches and some that have been previously dampened and a candle.

ACTIVITY AND APPLICATION:

Hold up a good match and ask: What great hidden power does it have? (Student choice.) How is it like a person's talent? (Student choice.) Now strike the match and light a candle. What does this match have the power to do? (It has the power to light and kindle other fires.) Now take a match that has been soaked in water and try to light it. It will just peel off without lighting. Ask: Why won't it light? (It has been dampened.) How are some peoples' talents like these two matches? (Student choice.) How are people's talents dampened before they start? (Many times a potentially good talent has been dampened by the actions of others, such as: Ridicule, disrespect, lack of consideration and rudeness.) Let us not dampen the talents of others by our actions. Help others develop their talents by our encouragement. They will then be able to use their talents to light and kindle the talents in others.

120

TEACHABLE

OBJECTIVE:

To illustrate how the spirit cannot enter when we close our minds or fill them with evil.

EQUIPMENT:

A glass science flask, a two-hole rubber stopper for the flask, a glass funnel and some food coloring.

ACTIVITY AND APPLICATION:

Put the glass funnel in one of the holes in the rubber stopper. Cover the other hole with your finger. Now try to pour some colored water into the funnel. Ask: Why won't it go into the flask? (The flask is full of air.) How can we get the water into the flask? (Student choice.) Now remove your finger from covering the hole and pour water into the funnel. Why does the water go through and into the flask now? The water forces the air out through the hole. The air inside the flask represents the ideas or philosophies of the world. The water represents the spirit of the Lord. The finger over the hole represents a closed mind. Why do we close our minds to the spirit of the Lord? (Student choice.)

What happens when we open our minds and are receptive to the spirit of the Lord? We have the power to drive out any evil that may be present because the spirit of the Lord is stronger.

TEACHING

OBJECTIVE:

To illustrate the value of growing up in the gospel from infancy.

EQUIPMENT:

A bottle with a full grown cucumber grown inside: Put an infant cucumber and its vine inside a narrow-necked bottle. Let it grow inside until full grown. Then cut off the vine and fill the bottle full of vinegar.

ACTIVITY AND APPLICATION:

Show the bottle with the cucumber in it and ask: How did this cucumber get into the bottle? There will be some who will not know. How do you think it got in? Clue: What is the only natural way it could get in? (It grew in the bottle as a young cucumber.) Now that it's in the bottle, how could you get it out? (Student choice.) You can't without breaking the bottle or destroying the content. What is the important lesson relating to the value of growing up with a spiritual background? (Student choice.) What is the meaning of this scripture: "Train up a child in the way he should go: and when he is old, he will not depart from it"? Proverbs 22:6 (Student choice.)

TEMPTATION

OBJECTIVE:

Demonstrate how sin is committed.

EQUIPMENT:

A large animal trap that is pre-set and a pencil.

ACTIVITY AND APPLICATION:

Show the animal trap and ask: Is there anyone who would dare put your finger in this trap? Now take the pencil and spring the trap, showing how the pencil is crushed. Reset the trap and ask: Would anyone put their finger in the trap in the same manner I did the pencil? If I put a $20 bill on the trigger, would you? What if I put a $50 bill on the trigger, would you then? How much would it take for you to put your finger into the trap the same way I put the pencil in? (Student choice.) Now demonstrate the following. Say: "No one would be so stupid as to put their finger right directly into this trap." Now put your finger on the outer rim of the trap and even near the trigger. Ask: But what will we do? (Student choice.) How is this like temptation? (Student choice.) How do we tamper with temptation? (We lie a little, cheat, neck, pet, play around with alcohol and tobacco and drugs.) What will eventually happen if we continue to tamper with any of these things? (Student choice.)

TESTIMONY

OBJECTIVE:

To illustrate the difference in peoples' testimonies.

EQUIPMENT:

Two candles, one with a dry wick, the other with a wet wick that has been soaked in water for a day.

ACTIVITY AND APPLICATION:

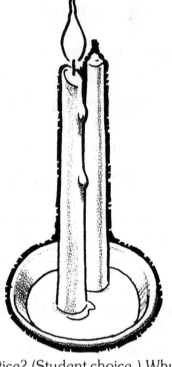

Ask the class to observe as you light both candles. Light the dry candle first, and then the wet candle. What difference did you notice? (Student choice.) Why did the first candle start so easy and shine steady and bright, while the other one flickered and sputtered? (The first is dry and the second is wet.) How is this like a person's testimony? (Student choice.) How are some testimonies dampened? (By sin, disobedience and lack of spiritual warmth.) What happened to the flickering candle as it continued to burn for awhile? It stopped flickering and burned steadily. What must a dampened testimony do before it will burn steadily? (Student choice.)

TESTIMONY

OBJECTIVE:

Demonstrate the value of living on your own light and not on borrowed light.

EQUIPMENT:

A regular flash light, and a special flash light called a "Dynamo" mf. by Spencer Gifts, Atlantic City, N.J. 08411.

ACTIVITY AND APPLICATION:

Turn out all the classroom lights. Turn on the regular flash light and explain: See, all I have to do is push a little switch and the light works. Turn off the regular flash light and show the special Dynamo, and explain: See, all I have to do is press this little handle, keep pressing it over and over, and see the light works. Ask: Which flash light would you like to have in an emergency? Why? (Student choice.) What is the meaning of the following statement? The time comes in our lives when we can no longer live on borrowed light; we must generate our own light. (Student choice.) What do we have within us that has the power to generate our own light? (Student choice.) We may live off another person's testimony for a time, but the time will come when we cannot live without our own testimony.

"THE ONE"

OBJECTIVE:

To illustrate the value of trying to save every soul in the kingdom of God.

EQUIPMENT:

Many keys of all different sizes and shapes on a ring and a door lock or some other lock that you have a key for.

ACTIVITY AND APPLICATION:

Demonstrate how only one of all the keys opens the lock. Say: It has been said "for every lock there is a key". What is the meaning of that statement as it relates to teaching? (Student choice.) How is getting into the heart of a student like these keys? (Student choice.) The worth of souls is great in the kingdom of our Father in Heaven. For every person we must try to find the key to open their heart and soul to the Lord.

THE ONE

OBJECTIVE:

To illustrate how teachers, parents and leaders need to get to the heart of their students and children.

EQUIPMENT:

Large egg-shaped styrofoam with a face painted on it, a raw egg and a glass.

ACTIVITY AND APPLICATION:

Show the class the large egg and say: "Hi, this is Eggbert. Some people think he's hard-boiled; not much to look at. They think he's kind of a tough egg to crack. But inside Eggbert, as inside each of you, is a golden part that needs to be found." Ask: How can this be done? (Crack it open.) (Now take the egg and crack it open.) What is it like inside? (Golden.) How do we crack Eggbert's shell? (You crack Eggbert's shell with a handshake, a warm smile and a spiritual atmosphere. Who are the Eggberts? (Student choice.) What is the golden part within a person? (Student choice.) Any student, even though he may be very hard-crusted or shelled, can be cracked open if the right kind of force is used.

TIME

OBJECTIVE:

To illustrate how we waste time every day.

EQUIPMENT:

A gallon bottle; enough small oranges to fill the bottle; and two quarts of water.

ACTIVITY AND APPLICATION:

Show the bottle and the oranges and say: This bottle represents a day. These oranges represent activities we may do in a day's time. What are some activities you do nearly every day? (Student choice.) Put the oranges into the bottle one at a time as each activity is mentioned by students. When all the oranges are in the bottle say: It's now full, and this represents a full day, right? No... Why doesn't it represent a full day? There's still space in between. Now pour the water into the bottle until it's full. What does this water represent? (Student choice.) What are some very important activities that we need to fit into every day? (Student choice.) Most of the time, when we think we have filled our day with meaningful activities, there is still much that could be done. We can make time during the day for important things such as: Prayer, scripture study and meditation.

TITHING

OBJECTIVE:

To illustrate that tithing means a tenth and nothing less.

EQUIPMENT:

Ten cookies on a plate.

ACTIVITY AND APPLICATION:

Before class begins select one student, and give him the following instructions: I will ask you to come to the front of the class, and will give you ten cookies. I will then ask you to give me one of them back. Don't give it back without some effort on my part. Then reluctantly give me one. But before you do, take a couple of bites out of it. Now demonstrate the above to the class. This demonstration is a clue to our topic, what do you think it is? (Tithing.) How is this demonstration like the way some people pay their tithing? (Student choice.) Why should he be willing to give me one cookie without so much effort on my part? (Student choice.) Where did he get all the cookies? (From me) Why should we be willing to give the Lord one tenth of our increase? The Lord gives us every thing we have, he even provides a way for us to make all the money we do, and then asks us to give just one tenth. However, like the cookies, many are not willing to do so until they have taken a couple of bites out of the Lord's tenth. What are some of the "bites" we take out of the Lord's tenth? (Student choice.)

TRAINING

OBJECTIVE:

To show the power and strength that training a child in his infancy has.

EQUIPMENT:

A china dish with a colored pattern.

ACTIVITY AND APPLICATION:

Show a china dish and demonstrate how you can't scrape the pattern off. Use a pocket knife or a key to scrape the dish. Ask: Why can't the pattern be removed? How did it get in there? (It has been inscribed and then baked in a furnace.) If you want to rub anything off, when must it be done? (You must rub it off while it is in the biscuit form.) What lesson does this teach us about training children? (Student choice.) When is the best time to change attitude and behavior? When children come to us they are in the biscuit form. We can inscribe on them what we please and "...they will not depart from it..." Proverbs 22:6.

TRIALS

OBJECTIVE:

Our reaction to hardship and trials depends upon our spiritual depth.

EQUIPMENT:

Two small birthday candles, one regular and one party fun-type. that keeps burning and comes back on after being blown out. These can be purchased from fun and magic shops.

ACTIVITY AND APPLICATION:

Show and light both candles and explain that they represent two people. Observe what qualities in people both candles represent. When the party candle starts to sparkle a little, blow the regular candle out gently, and then blow out the party candle gently. Blow them both out gently or the party candle may not come back on. Both candles were blown out by the same amount of force. But why did one come back on? (It has something inside that keeps it going.) In life how are people like these two candles when faced with equal amounts of trials? (Student choice.) What is it that some people have inside them that keeps them going and they don't lose faith when hardship hits?

(Student choice.) According to I Cor. 10:13, we all have equal trials and hardships in this life. When some get hit by the winds and storms of life, their light goes out because they don't have what it takes inside to keep them going. They have a weakness in their testimony. A good example of this is Nephi versus Laman and Lemuel.

TRUTH

OBJECTIVE:

Demonstrate how you cannot change absolute truth.

EQUIPMENT:

An overhead projector, several small objects such as: Chalk, bolt, coin, nail, battery, button and bullet.

ACTIVITY AND APPLICATION:

Place the above objects on the overhead projector, standing them on their end or side. Put something in front and around the sides of the projector to block the vision, so students can't see the objects. Turn on the projector and ask students to identify as many of the objects as they can. Next lay the objects down one by one and let the students identify them. Why couldn't all the objects be identified at first but could be when we laid them down? (Student choice.) The position of the object didn't change the truth. Why is truth so hard for some people to see? (Student choice.) How do Satan and evil men make familiar objects take on a more attractive appearance? Even obvious things become hard to recognize. But what can never be changed? (Truth.) Why? (Student choice.)

TWO MASTERS

OBJECTIVE:

To demonstrate the problem of trying to serve two masters.

EQUIPMENT:

Two clear drinking straws, some food coloring and a glass of water.

ACTIVITY AND APPLICATION:

Fill the glass full of drinking water and mix some food coloring with it. Put one straw in the glass, and show how easy it is to suck up a little water. Now put one straw inside the glass and the other straw outside the glass. Try drinking the water with the same amount of force you used with the first straw. With the same amount of effort why can't I get any water? (Student choice.) How does this demonstration relate to Jesus' advice in Matt. 6:24, "No man can serve two masters..."? (Student choice.)

VIRTUE

OBJECTIVE:

To illustrate how purity causes evil to flee. James 4:7

EQUIPMENT:

A glass pie plate half full of water, pepper shaker, liquid soap, and an overhead projector.

ACTIVITY AND APPLICATION:

Place the glass pie plate half full of water on the overhead projector. Turn on the projector and sprinkle pepper all over the surface of the water. The pepper represents Satan or evil. Drop one drop of liquid soap in the center of the water. Watch the pepper separate. What made the pepper separate and flee to the ouside? (Soap.) What does soap represent? (Cleanser, purity.) What does this illustration represent in life? (Student choice.) What will always make Satan flee? According to I Nephi 15:34, how do we rid ourselves of filth? (The kingdom of God is not filthy.) In James 4:7 what happens when we submit ourselves to God? (We will be able to resist the devil and he will flee from us.)

WITNESSES

OBJECTIVE:

To demonstrate the value of the testimony of two witnesses.

EQUIPMENT:

A peanut.

ACTIVITY AND APPLICATION:

With the peanut in your hand, raise your hand before the class and make the following statement: "I have something in my hand that has never, ever been touched by human hands. How many of you believe me?" Next show the nut to a student in private and ask him to testify to the class that my statement is true. Ask: how many believe? Show a second student the nut and ask student to testify the same as the first student did. (By this time most students should believe.) Why do you believe now? (Student choice.) Ask the two student witnesses: "Could you ever honestly deny what you saw?" Why is the statement of these two students so important? (Student choice.) What is the law of the witnesses? "In the mouth of two or three witnesses may every word be established." Matt. 18:16.

WORK

OBJECTIVE:

To demonstrate how work and activity increase our strength.

EQUIPMENT:

A magnet hanging from the ceiling with metal attached to it.

ACTIVITY AND APPLICATION:

Relate the following: A magnet was seen in a chemist's laboratory, suspended against the wall, and loaded heavily with weights. The visitors wanted to know why. Ask: Why do you think it was? (Student choice.) The answer is: The scientist said the magnet was losing its power by lying around without being used, so they were restoring its force by giving it something to do. In this same way, how are people like magnets? (Student choice.) It is with man as with magnets. Idleness and inactivity result in loss of power. To him who uses what he has, shall be given more. The secret to restored force is to have something worthwhile to do.

WORSHIP

OBJECTIVE:

To show how just being a member of the Church is not enough. Only by living the gospel as taught by the Church can we receive any benefit.

EQUIPMENT:

Two signs reading: I am a Mormon. To the first sign, attach a string with a loop to go over the neck. Also attach a nice fresh carrot and a potato so it hangs down below the sign. Make the second sign like the first, except attach a dried up carrot and potato to this one.

ACTIVITY AND APPLICATION:

Wear the first sign and ask: What do you think this represents? (Student choice.) What is the relationship between wearing the food and wearing the sign? (Student choice.) What good or potential does the food contain? (Nourishment to the physical body.) What is the good or potential of the Church? (It gives nourishment to the spirit.) What will happen if we just wear the food? (Student choice.) Now show the second sign and ask: How are some members of the church like this? (Student choice.) The Church gives nourishment to the spirit when we take the gospel into our souls by drinking of the "Living Water". Neither the food nor the Church will nourish us if we just wear them.

YOUTH

OBJECTIVE:

To illustrate the positive potential of youth.

EQUIPMENT:

Stamped envelope, ink blotter, sand paper, flash bulb and a balloon.

ACTIVITY AND APPLICATION:

Say: It is a pleasure to work and be associated with the great youth of the Church. It is also very interesting. I will illustrate the way some people feel about them. Show each of the following objects and ask: How are some youth like:

1. A postage stamp? You have to lick them before they'll work.

2. An ink blotter? They soak it all up backwards.

3. Sand paper? They always give you a rough time.

4. Flash bulb? They flash

bright only once.

    5. A balloon? They are full of hot air.

However, I believe that they all have great potential, and like the following objects, they have positive qualities. How are these youth like the positive qualities of:

    1. A Stamp? Even though you have to lick them to make them work, they always stick there until their job is finished.

    2. An ink blotter? Even though they may soak it up backwards, they soak up a lot of problems.

    3. Sand paper? They may give you a rough time, but there's nothing like them to make a rough surface smooth.

    4. A flash bulb? It flashes bright only once, but it works when nothing else will.

    5. A balloon? They may be full of hot air, but they have so many uses and great flexibility.

Look for the positive characteristics in youth; their potential is great.

JESUS IS OUR MODEL TEACHER

The parables and teachings of Jesus are not only interesting and thought provoking, but are highly applicable to man and his spiritual achievement and social relationship today.

Human nature has not changed since the days of Adam. Those things that made man fit for the kindgom of God in earlier ages make men fit for the kingdom today. Men learn new methods, but the underlying urges, hopes, temptations, principles, and challenges are the same now as always. Man's relationship to his fellow men and to God has not changed. Thus gospel principles emphasized by Jesus are as sorely needed and just as effective today as at any time. The teaching methods of Jesus were responses to real situations and were spoken to meet definite needs. They were tailored to the event and spoken with a purpose. In setting forth gospel principles from various symbolisms, Jesus used object lessons. He made reference to and comparison with many objects in the form of people, places and things. The following is a list of over 200 objects used by Jesus in setting forth gospel principles. This list is taken from the four gospels, starting with his formal ministry and ending just before his crucifixion.

Altar, ashes, arm, bags, bank, barns, barley, beam, bed, beggar, belly, birds, blind, blood, body, bones, bramblebush, bread, bride, bridechamber, bridegroom, burglars, bushel, candle, candlestick, camel, cattle, child, chickens, clay, clothing, cloak, closets, cloud, coat, compass, corn, creditor, cup, darkness, deaf, debtors, den, ditch, dinner, dogs, door, doves, drink, dust, ears, egg, eye of needle, farthings, figs, fig tree, fire, fish, fishes, fisherman, fishers, flocks, flowers, flood, fold, foot, footstool, foundation, fountain, fowls, fox, foxes, fruits, furnace, gate, gift, gluttonous, gnat, goats, goods, grapes, grass, graves, ground, grinding, hair, hand, harvest, heart, hedges, hen, hireling, highwaymen, holes, house, housetop, husbandmen, infants, laborers, lambs, leaven, light, lilies, linen, lion, mammon, mansions, market, meal, meat, merchant, millstone, mite, money, mote, mountains, mustard seed, napkin, nest, net, needle, new cloth, new wine, night, oil, old bottles, old garments, oven, ox, oxen, path, pearls, pence, penny, Pharisees, physician, pigs, pipe, pit, plant, platter, plough, pool, poor, porter, pounds, prince, prison, publican, queen, raiment, rain, ravens, reapers, reed, riches, robes, robber, rocks, roots, sackcloth, salt, sand, scorpions, Scribes, sea, seeds, serpents, sign, sheep, sheepfold, shepherd, sky, silver, sifter, smoking flax, snare, soft raiment, sop, sower, sowing, sparrows, stall, strait gate, stripes, stone, storehouse, sunsets, supper, swine, sycamore tree, talents, tares, teeth, temple, thief, thistles, threshing grain, thorns, tower, treasure, tree, trumpet, vessels, vine, vineyard, vipers, virgins, water, waterpots, wayside, wedding, well, wheat, wine, wings, widow, wilderness, worm, wolves, yoke.

WHEN SELECTING AND USING OBJECT LESSONS

When selecting object lessons for teaching it is a good idea to keep in mind how and why Jesus used them. The following suggestions are based on experiences in the classroom the setting and surroundings of Jesus' sermons and teachings in the Holy land.

1. His objects were always familiar to the people and the location.

2. The objects were simple and easy to understand.

3. The gospel application could easily be made by his faithful listeners.

4. The object must be easily visible to students.

5. Jesus always used objects to teach a gospel principle.

6. The listeners participated through question and answers.

7. Jesus used objects to teach lessons on a current issue or problem.

8. Object lessons are very effective as motivators introducing lessons and clinching important concepts.

Object lessons are an effective method of teaching for the following reasons:

1. They are immediate attention getters.

2. They help students think and learn by self-discovery of gospel applications.

3. They offer enrichment, spice and variety to the lesson.

4. Students remember the object and will be able to make their own application.

5. The method is fun and exciting for the teacher, helping him develop the "growing edge" as he thinks of new ideas and gospel applications.

6. Students enjoy object lessons.

HOW TO CREATE AND USE YOUR OWN OBJECT LESSONS

Ideas for object lessons come from many sources. The following are some examples:

SCRIPTURES -- See page 62 of this book for the gospel application and object lesson of Matt. 5:13, 14;

CONFERENCE ADDRESS--See page 103 of this book for an example.

SONGS--See page 24 of this book for the example.

POETRY--See page 76 of this book for an example.

STORIES--See page 74 of this book for an example.

SCIENCE EXPERIMENTS--See page 93 of this book for an example.

QUOTATIONS--See page 59 of this book for an example.

YOUR OWN CREATIVITY--In creating your own object lessons, first keep your eyes open and search for interesting objects such as: Animal traps, magnets, compass, old tools, antiques, etc. Start a collection of these and other really special objects. You can find a gospel application to most any object. There are many places to find objects: On the farm, in barns, sheds and work shops; at farm auctions, antique shops, gift, fun and hobby shops, magic stores. A really good source is to ask your students to bring you interesting objects.

How do you make gospel applications from object lessons? First, you do just like Jesus did--you make comparisons. In making comparisons, think of all the things that the object does and stands for. Then think of the gospel principles or concepts that fit the comparison. We will illustrate how to do this by using the large animal trap as the object:

OBJECT--What it does and stands for 1. ANIMAL TRAP	Gospel Comparisons
A. Used by trappers to catch animals.	Satan uses Traps to catch people.
B. The bait is used to lure animals.	People are lured by evil and conspiring men, by social pressure and by colorful ads.
C. The trap represents injury or death to the animal.	If men are caught in Satan's trap, it means death also. Maybe slow physical, but immediate spiritual death.
D. Animals get caught in the trap by first sniffing cautiously, then nibbling, and finally biting,	Men do not break the commandments all at once; they go through temptation, luring, thought, and then try to get away with just a little.
E. Once an animal is caught, the trap is vicious and the trapper takes no mercy on his victim.	Satan's only reward is to make men miserable like himself, he has no mercy on his captives. (Alma 30:60)

Try this procedure on a few easy simple objects around the house, such as: The radio, electric iron, flour sifter, potato peeler, soap, building tools, thermometer and many others. A good object may be used to teach several gospel topics. Those in this book could be adapted to fit other gospel topics by following the above procedure.

The actual use and presentation of an object lesson in a class situation can be a most enjoyable experience for the teacher as well as the students if presented skillfully.

In most situations we need to try to draw the gospel applications out of the students by letting them see the comparisons and then letting them fill in the gospel meanings. This can be done in several ways:

1. You may just show an ojbect and ask students to tell everything that it represents according to a specific gospel topic. For example: Soap is the object. And repentance is the topic. The application is that both are cleansers if used properly.

2. You may show an object and ask the students what major gospel topics could be represented by it. When the topic that you are teaching is suggested, you ask: In what ways does this object represent the topic. Then talk about all the applications.

3. You may ask the students to merely observe as you give a demonstration and then have the class suggest all the gospel truths that are represented by the demonstration.

4. You may use the inquiry method. This is having students discover the specific lesson by means of asking the teacher questions that can be answered with

just a "yes", or "no" answer. As they ask the questions, you lead them to the lesson. You may need to give small clues and review what has been learned along the way. Show an object or give a demonstration and ask students to discover its gospel meaning by use of the inquiry method. You may need to teach them the inquiry method before beginning.

Regardless of the method used to present the object lesson, make sure you TEACH and not just TELL.

NEIL W. DECKER

Much of Neil Decker's life has been devoted to teaching professionally as a seminary instructor and in the Church in many ward and stake capacities. He served a full-time mission to the Northwestern States. He received his bachelor's degree from Weber State College, and a master's degree in recreation Education from BYU. Brother Decker spent eight years in the Army Reserve, serving much of the time as acting chaplain. He loves life and is at the height of enjoyment when having a good time with the youth in classroom or recreational activities.

When Brother Decker started teaching seminary in the little town of Duchesne, Utah his greatest desire was to become a successful seminary teacher. "What makes a good lesson?" he asked the students. "We've seen a few object lessons and really enjoyed those

148

classes." "What's an object lesson?" he then asked. From their responses inspiration for many object lessons had its beginning. With this unique ability to see or think of objects that have gospel applications, or teach topics by finding objects that are "...like unto them..." Brother Decker has created a storehouse of object lessons.

Brother Decker and his wife Sharon now reside on a small acreage in Eagle, Idaho. They have six children: Shanell, Wendy, Benjamin, Lisa, Aaron and Amy.